MW01712317

What's *Your* EXCUSE?

By Michael Saunders

No Excuses Needed; Heb. 12:2

Michael Saunders

ZOË LIFE PUBLISHING
WORDS TO LIVE BY

Published by:
Zoë Life Publishing
P.O. Box 871066
Canton, MI 48187 USA
www.zoelifepub.com

Definitions used were taken from:
Genuine Merriam-Webster Dictionary

Take note that the name satan and associated names are not capitalized. We choose not to give him any preeminence, even to the point of violating grammatical rules.

Author:	Michael Saunders
Cover Designer:	Chamira Jones
Editor:	Jessica Colvin

First U.S. Edition Year 1st Edition was Published

Library of Congress Cataloging-in-Publication Data

Saunders, Michael.
What's your excuse? / by Michael Saunders.
p. cm.
Includes bibliographical references and index.
ISBN-13: 978-1-934363-09-6
ISBN-10: 1-934363-09-X
1. Apologetics. I. Title.
BT1103.S38 2007
239--dc22
2007044571

Saunders, Michael

What's Your Excuse?

Summary: What *does* it mean to be a Christian? In *What's Your Excuse*, Michael Saunders uncovers and de-bunks all the "myths" that non-believers use as justification for not turning to God, as well as, answering many of the questions that new believers are afraid or embarrassed to ask.

10 Digit ISBN 1-934363-09-X
13 Digit ISBN 978-1-934363-09-6

For current information about releases by Michael Saunders or other releases from Zoë Life Publishing, visit our web site: htttp://www.zoelifepub.com

Printed in the United States of America

V7 01 15 08

Dedication

This book is dedicated to all who find themselves looking at others, as they search for reasons to justify their excuses for their denial of the Gospel of Jesus Christ. This is a condition which plagues many people, and I was one of them for much of my life. This book is written largely out of my own familiarity with the search for reinforcement of our mistaken beliefs based on examples of believers we have met. My goal is to show how this attitude could very well lead you into eternal separation from God, and to encourage you to ask God, with everything in your soul, not to let that happen to you, or anyone you love.

Lastly, it is dedicated to my wife, Denise. She stood beside me, and encouraged me to keep going whenever the enemy tried to convince me I was "out of my league." He was right, but God makes me what I am, and there is nothing beyond His guidance! My wife never scoffed at the idea of my writing, and was there for me throughout this project. Denise, I thank you for all of your encouragement and love. You have helped lead me to the completion of this book, and have given me the courage to share it with the public. To God be the Glory! Amen.

A Special Thank You

I have three people I'd like to say a very special thank you to, who were instrumental in my completing this book and bringing it to a publisher for consideration. The first is to my dear friend Scott, who encouraged me to begin the project over a dinner conversation. At the time, I know neither one of us had any idea it would go as far as it has—at least I know I didn't—he might disagree. Thank you, Scott, for believing in me even when I didn't believe in myself.

The next thank you goes out to our youth pastor, Pastor Jim (PJ to our teens). Jim, your friendship has meant more than I can say in my following through on this project. You have been ever encouraging, and helped keep me focused on believing that I wasn't "out of my league" for undertaking this book. During the times when I felt discouraged, you always found some way to pick my spirits back up—and keep me moving forward. Thank you, Jim, for being my personal prayer warrior.

Lastly, I want to thank my dear friend Denise (my "other" Denise). I have missed you terribly since you retired, but I will never forget the mentoring you shared with me. You were responsible for my meeting Sabrina of Zoe Life Publishing, and I will be forever thankful. God worked through difficult health situations in both you and Sabrina to bring the two of you together, and then He brought you both to me years later. Thank you, Denise, for being such a dear friend.

What's *Your* EXCUSE?

By Michael Saunders

Table of Contents

Introduction

This book is written for anyone who has ever had an interest in exploring what it means to be a Christian, but has never made an honest effort of their own because there has always been a convenient excuse for you to use in dismissing your need for salvation; we shall call you the "explorers." It is also written for those of you who find yourselves trying to remain convinced you are already saved, but cannot find any evidence in your life to serve as proof of that fact; we shall call you the "saved but unsure." In this book, you will find the Biblical answers to many of these excuses for not allowing Jesus Christ to become both the Savior and Lord of your life. You will also find ways to gain assurance you truly have been saved if you continually experience doubt over your present place in God's kingdom. Finally, this book is written for those who desire to share their faith in a way that is intimate, relevant and appealing by living their faith out loud; we shall call them the "share or not to share" category.

Many of these excuses I used myself for dismissing Christianity from my life for many years. What I pray this book does for you is to reveal the truth through the Word of God that lead to my overcoming of these excuses, and that it will help you to do the same.

Many other excuses I have heard from friends I have talked with and the answers to them as found in God's Word have been placed here as well. I pray that, whatever your particular excuse might be, you will find it addressed here in this book or at the very least one similar enough to allow you to apply the answer to your own personal version of it.

Excuses are nothing more than illegitimate reasons we make up in our attempts to cover a wrong-doing in our lives.

When it comes to using them for the purpose of covering our denial of our Lord Jesus Christ, His message of salvation, His Lordship, or sharing our faith; they become the worst thing we could ever allow to exist in our lives. It is my prayer this book will help you to see that the "reasons" we use for denying Christ's message, are really nothing more than excuses we have created or allowed others to create for us. Once we get to the point where we recognize them for what they truly are, then we are much better prepared to overcome them and consider Christ with an open heart and an honest perspective. Read this book prayerfully, and I believe you will be blessed with insight and revelation that will change your outlook on God and His Church for the rest of your life.

This book is also written for the person who believes they already have a personal relationship with Christ but they cannot see any evidence of that relationship in their daily walk. It may be you are someone who truly wants to be a member of God's family, but you just aren't sure. You may believe you are saved based on something you have learned or heard from others, but you are unsure of your own true state of salvation because of those nagging feelings of doubt and the feeling there is something still not quite right in your life. If this is the condition you find yourself in, then you will be blessed through reading the descriptions of what salvation means and how to go about receiving it.

The third group of people for whom this book is written, is the group who wants to lead others to a meaningful relationship with God, through His Son, Jesus; but are looking for help in how to share their faith effectively with them. If you need some ideas on what you can say to your friends when they ask you about God and His Church, or when they ask you how you know you are saved, or they want to know what the Bible says about why they are here, and most importantly how to live your faith out loud, it is my prayer that I have provided you with all this and more. You will find a simple description of what God's Word says about questions like these, and where to find the answers when you need them.

When God gave the inspiration to the authors of the books of the Bible, He told them to write in such a way that everyone and anyone who read them would understand; I pray that the words contained in this book are also written in this way and with the idea that God so loved the world, that He sent His only begotten Son that we may understand and know the love of God.

I love to read books that help me to live a Christian life, but I have found most of them tend to be written to people who already have a higher understanding of theology, Christianity, and religion. I was inspired to write a book that talked about the questions we all have about God and His kingdom, in a way that was easy to understand with answers in everyday language, to everyday questions, for everyday people. I wrote this book with many prayers and hours sitting at the feet of Jesus, and I urge you to read it in the same way. Pray for God to send His Spirit to touch your heart and your mind as you read this book, so you may be granted the understanding, insight, and revelation that are intended for you in these pages.

I pray God will bless you with the greatest gift He has ever offered to mankind; eternal life with Him and His Son in His heavenly kingdom. I wrote each page with the hope of you receiving and sharing this precious gift.

As you go forward in reading this book, I just want to once more encourage you to please read prayerfully. Anytime you read the Holy Bible or anything written about God's Word, always ask God for help first. Help in clearly seeing what is expressed in the written word, this brings understanding and understanding brings revelation. Revelation is when God reveals the true intent of His Word to your heart. He can make His Word real to you. If you will apply that same principle to the reading of this book or any other written to serve God and His kingdom, you will be blessed with more understanding than you could ever gain in your own strength. Remember this one principle always; prayer before seeking knowledge. Pray for understanding, pray for clarity, pray for discernment and pray for revelation. God Bless...

1

Why Aren't You a Christian?

The Excuses

Chapter One

I'm Just as "Religious" as He Is

The question I discuss in the first section of this book is: why aren't you a Christian? There are so many different excuses people give in response, and I am going to share some of them with you.

The most common excuse, by far, people give is that they see no real reason to consider a commitment to God. They see themselves as already being as "religious" as the Christians they have encountered in their lives. This is a frightening statement, and a condemnation on many of us who profess ourselves to be Christians.

These types of "religious" Christians create an enormous problem because they contribute to the "hypocrite" excuse. I was tempted to throw my hands up in the air when I began to realize the size and scope of the problem. But, knowing there is nothing which God cannot overcome, I press onward as I try to understand the problem more thoroughly. It is only through investigation and understanding, that we will be able to find a solution.

Just as you peel away the layers of an onion, so must we peel away the examples of these "religious" people we encounter in our walks. When you get to the very core of the problem, it is hypocrisy being observed by our fellow citizens in this world. To be absolutely clear on what hypocrisy really is, let's look at a definition for it as given in the Webster's Dictionary; "A feigning to be something which one is not or to believe something which one does not."

Hypocrisy in Christianity has formed a gulf so wide, it seems almost impossible to do anything about it. For man by himself, it would be impossible. But opening up God's Word, we can find encouragement in Mark 10:27; "Jesus looked at them and said, 'With man this is impossible, but not with God; all things are possible with God.'" Praise God for His written Word! It not only provides us with the answers we seek, but also gives the encouragement we need to handle them. In the case of hypocrisy in the Christian Church, part of the problem lies in the fact the world refuses to accept any of the differences between self-professing Christians who live contrary to true Christian values, and those who truly exemplify the life that Jesus Christ called for us to live.

Jesus taught us about the way we should see our lives as Christians, and the way we should live them based upon our new understanding as believers. The basic principles of a believer's life are outlined in His Sermon on the Mount, which is found in the book of Matthew 5, 6, & 7; I will be sharing from this sermon throughout this book. When it comes to seeing the differences between Christians who are trying to follow these Biblical principles and those who are not, the world prefers to relish in the fact it has this group of contradictory

Christians to use in its attacks against the Christian Church as a whole.

When facing this problem of hypocrisy, a verse like the one we looked at from the book of Mark can help us to not feel completely helpless and without hope. Hypocrisy is a problem of such magnitude, it threatens to destroy any sense of resistance we may have in addressing it. But true Christians are not just a group of lackluster failures, who stand by and watch this world as it slips into oblivion. We have a mighty God who promises to help us in all things!

Even now, I am being tempted by satan to stop this foolishness of trying to put my thoughts and observations down on paper! Who do you think you are? Who do you think will ever read them? Do you honestly believe you can write something worthwhile for anybody to consider? These questions keep coming to me as doubts, and I know it is the devil who plants them in my heart and mind!

You who are reading these words, have you ever had the same experience when contemplating some endeavor of your own? Have you ever tried to make a definite decision to accomplish something for the Lord, only to find in the end that you never completed whatever it was you started? How many of us have been stifled by these thoughts of uselessness we just can't seem to rid ourselves of?

I have been shut down before, but through much prayer and determination, this time I shall press on towards completion of this project I find myself drawn to! It is so easy to be a dreamer of dreams, thinking briefly of ideas sounding so good at the beginning. It is in following through on the work required when we are so easily deterred. This time, I shall draw upon the strength of the Lord so I can accomplish the task set before me, just as we are shown in example from

2 Timothy 4:7; "I have fought the good fight, I have finished the race, I have kept the faith."

Pressing on towards the goal I have set for myself, I will begin by peeling off some of these layers we find in our midst of the body we collectively call the Christian Church. We must first try to understand the gigantic size of this group of people. The secular world places so many different groups into this category, it is hard to determine the actual amount of people included.

For the basis of this book, I place here the Biblical prerequisites one must meet in order to consider themselves to be a Christian. First of all, you must believe Jesus Christ is the only Son of the Living God. That He was virgin-born, and lived a sin-free life while here on earth. You must believe He was crucified on the Cross for our sins, and that He was raised from the dead three days later; conquering death. You must be convicted of your sins, turn from them in repentance, and ask Jesus to receive you as one of His own. After publicly doing this, you should be baptized into the Body of Christ; which is called His Church.

In some denominations, there can be some additional areas they may teach you need to fulfill, and in others there may be a few less than these I listed. For the purposes of this book, consider those listed as the basic guidelines which the Bible specifically expresses. These fundamental guidelines will be shared in great detail throughout this book, and I will share why I believe they are the essential elements of the Christian faith.

Now, when looking at these so-called hypocritical Christians, I see them falling into three different categories. There are three different layers, just like an onion. The deeper you get into them, the more they tend to burn your eyes. The outer layer is the easiest to remove, and the most obvious. On the onion, part of this first layer is open and not completely attached. This layer is exposed to the eye without even trying to peel it off. It is actually difficult not to see this layer if you make any effort whatsoever; it is the same way with this first layer of hypocritical believers.

1st Layer: The Easy To Spot Hypocrite

I am going to categorize this first layer of hypocritical Christians as the "easy to spot" variety. It does not take much effort at all to notice them. There are many traits and characteristics they have in common, and all of these have been used by people trying to explain their reasons for not considering the Christian life. After all, we must admit that most people can truthfully claim to lead a life which is just as "religious" as the lives these hypocritical Christians lead.

One of the common traits in the people of the "easy to spot" variety is how they usually attend services at some sort of church or religious establishment. This is a trend found in all three of the different layers, as we shall see later. However, in this outer-most layer, we most often discover their attendance tends to be sporadic at best. For them it is not the frequency which matters in this area; simply the ability to be able to claim they are "church-goers." They can be the people who attend during what we could call the "holi"-days of the year; Christmas, Easter, Mother's Day, and any other days they may think are the "special" ones.

There is no requirement for them to be active in their chosen establishment; simply the ability to say they have attended is enough. For many members of this group, it may prove to be that they merely attended some youth outreach program of a church when they were children. That alone can be enough to satisfy their sense of belonging to the Christian culture. Some of them may even take it a step further. As long as they have sent or are currently sending their own children to one of these programs, then that is enough to justify their claims to Christendom.

To take it even one step further, some of them believe if their own parents have fulfilled one or more of these situations, then that is enough to qualify for their own claims as well. The connection of Christianity through family involvement at one time or another is often exploited for the purposes of this claim to belong in the Family of God.

We can find that even this thin connection to some type of church affiliation is not necessarily required for an individual to lay a claim to Christianity. There are some who take it to an even more obscure association in that they simply need to be part of a certain ethnic background in order to lay their claims down. There are still more individuals who, when asked if they are a Christian, will respond without any hesitation that they are—wholly on the basis of having been born in this country or that one. It does not seem to bother them when they cannot provide any justification for their claim to believe in the Scriptures. The fact they claim it is enough for them, and they believe others should accept it, too.

The world has no problem, whatsoever, accepting this notion of belonging to Christendom on these grounds of race, origin, or any other quality. The world is only all too happy to make whatever allowances necessary to include anybody into this collective group of people who are termed "religious." Whenever something suits the true desires of the world's secular agenda, it is always ready to help in any way possible to achieve the end desired and longed for.

It is important to realize that the secular world is an active partner in this battle for recognition as being "religious" by definition. The world is constantly adding fuel to the fire burning in the hearts of those who wish to believe they are as good and moral as those who call themselves Christian. That is a big part of the problem we are dealing with here; the perception that anybody who claims they are Christian is accepted as being so without any litmus tests being applied to their declaration.

This simple step of merely being in some way or another connected to some form of religious organization, no matter how vague it may appear, is only one of the characteristics shared by many in this group of "easy to spot" variety of hypocritical Christians. Another trait I have experienced from this group is the way they tend to spend a great deal of time tearing down other people who claim to be Christian; but, also believe there should be some sort of evidence of your faith observed in your lifestyle. Most commonly, the "easy to spot" types will name-call to tear others down. They'll use words like: fundamental, narrow-minded, bigoted, self-righteous, old-fashioned, legalistic, and many other titles to make these Bible-following Christians unacceptable in the public's eye. If a particular denomination chooses to follow the guidelines and principles as set forth in God's Word, then this "easy to spot" group attacks that church relentlessly.

It is in this process of destroying the credibility of a Bible preaching church, where we find the secular world so quick to run to the aid of its attackers. Just read any of the mainstream newspapers, or watch any of the television news services to see if this claim is true. Although reporting the news is meant only to convey the facts about events as they occur, it takes no great effort to see that the secular press is an active partner in the agenda of tearing down the Bible-based Christian Church.

Examples of this fact are easily found. One such instance would be the way the media heralded the appointment of an openly homosexual man as a bishop of the Episcopalian Church. Not only were other denominations denounced when they voiced their opposition to this mockery of Biblical doctrine, but members of the Episcopal Church itself, who stood against this act, were also ridiculed for being bigoted and narrow-minded. The favorite catch phrase of the secularists is to call such people the religious, right-wing radicals.

There are many such examples in our papers and on our news broadcasts every day. It is not difficult to confirm my claim of this agenda for the systematic defamation of the Christian Church as a practice which is truly happening. In reality, it would be much more of a challenge to disprove it.

The saddest effect of this struggle, which is perceived by the world's population as a battle within the Church itself, is that it makes it much more difficult for anyone to make an educated decision as to what they want to believe. It becomes almost an impossibility to determine what Christianity truly stands for when there are so many voices in direct contradiction with each other. The end result is mass confusion; which often appears to be the desired outcome.

Another way this group of hypocritical Christians seeks to elevate themselves into acceptance is to shout about the failings of the fundamentalists. This takes very little effort, as members of both groups are merely human. Who among us does not make mistakes, which can easily be pointed out as contradictory to Christian beliefs? If a prominent evangelical is found to be involved in some misgiving such as sexual immorality, illegal drug use, financial misdealing, or any other downfall; they are held up like some sort of trophy for all to see.

This is one of the most damaging areas for God's Church when it is used to showcase the hypocrisy to be found throughout. It does not matter if these instances may be few and far between. It does not matter if the individuals involved may be truly repentant. The end result is the justification by many to claim they are proven once again to be as "religious" as anyone else who claims to be a Christian.

This is one of the easiest situations for this layer to exploit, and they will use any one from within their own ranks to achieve their goal. This proves itself to be an easy accomplishment since there are so many claiming to be Christian, but refusing to live by Biblical principles. This makes examples of downfall easily found, and the process has taken on a life of its own in a continual firestorm of man's failings.

As we saw in the other traits of this layer of "easy to spot" hypocrites; the secular media and news organizations need no prodding to help bring the downfalls of Christian men and women to the forefront of society. I feel kind of silly even bothering to point this fact out to you, since you would have to live on another planet to not be aware of that truth. It is one of the so-called facts of life which sadden me the most; but it is part of the reality in which we are currently living. Only by living the Christian life as God describes it in His Word do we have any hope of trying to correct this current state of the world in which we live.

There are other traits to be found in this layer I call the "easy to spot" variety, but these traits can also be found in the next two varieties we are going to look at. The most common observation with these traits I have pointed out to start, is their ease in being noticed when you simply look for them.

2nd Layer: The Well-Concealed Hypocrite

I call this second layer of hypocritical Christians the "well concealed" variety. Although they share many of the same traits as the "easy to spot" variety, there are some subtle differences between them which make them a little more difficult to recognize. At first glance, they appear to be very much Christian in the way they live their lives. To see if they are what they seem to be, we need to take a deeper look into their behavior and determine if they truly are living a life that follows the standards which God has set up for us.

One obvious characteristic of this group is that they will almost always be members of some sort of church. One of the differences between them and the "easy to spot" variety is in that they will not attend only on special occasions or "holi"-days. These "well-concealed" individuals are usually regular church attendees, and they are usually involved in the activities of their churches.

In most cases, there isn't any single trait standing out as a warning that something is not quite as it should be with this type of person. They are usually well versed in Bible Scripture, and they tend to be better educated in this area than many Christians who truly exhibit the qualities as outlined in our Bible. It is not through failure to know God's Word where they show their lack of true commitment; it is more in their failure to live the life of which they profess to be living.

Only by spending time in fellowship with these individuals will you be able to notice there is something not quite as it should be. It is both a sad thing, and a blessing, when we are able to notice the inconsistencies which are present in the lives of these "religious" hypocrites.

The problem lies in the guidelines our Lord stated clearly

in His Sermon on the Mount. It is impossible for any person to follow them without the Holy Spirit as their guide, and that is the predicament in which these people find themselves trapped. It is only after we have truly accepted Jesus as our Lord and Savior, that the Holy Spirit enters our lives, and enables us to follow these guidelines.

This is the test of faith our Lord supplied for us to use. It is this standard which gives us the ability to recognize those subtle differences between true Christian followers and people claiming to be Christians, but who fail to display the traits which we are told will be present in His children. To be sure, we all fail at some point while living this Christian life, but the difference will be in the pattern of life choices. Although failing at times, the truly Christian individual will always strive to recover. With renewed strength, they grow closer and closer to becoming a follower as described in God's Word.

An individual may appear to exhibit Christian qualities, but in time spent with them, their true characteristics always show through. In many cases, it will be something as simple as the usage of vulgar and coarse language. This practice is one of the things secular society is making every allowance for. The legal system is removing laws which were written against committing this type of offensive behavior in public places; thereby removing the word "offensive" from the definition of vulgar language.

God's Word tells believers not to use this type of language, and we can read what He said in Ephesians 5:4–5:

> Nor should there be obscenity, foolish talk, or coarse joking, which are out of place, but rather thanksgiving. For of this you can be sure: No immoral, impure or

greedy person—such a man is an idolater—has any inheritance in the kingdom of Christ and of God.

It does not matter if man wants to say obscenities are no longer bad; God's Word does.

The all too common practice of sharing what are called "off color" jokes is another example of this type of behavior. This is a method used to spread much more than just foul language. Many use this method to push their agendas of racism, bigotry, sexual immorality, and other similarly disgusting subjects. It is sad when you hear a professing Christian sharing in this way. It is sadder still when they try to justify and excuse their behavior with comments like, "It was just all in fun, no big deal, no harm-no foul, and finally; can't you take a joke?"

Anybody who reads those words from Ephesians will never be able to stand before God and say they didn't know it was wrong to talk in that way. My friend, it is wrong. It's wrong because God says it is wrong. It will never matter how many people collectively decide it is not wrong; God does not change, and neither do right and wrong. If you are professing to be a believer, think hard on the effects of such behavior on the unsaved that are watching and listening to you.

The use of foul language is a more obvious example of hypocritical behavior on the part of professing believers; another example can be seen in their personalities. Does someone have an appearance of being angry much of the time? Do they seem to be miserable about their life? Is there an absence of joy in their personality? These are character traits which are common in unbelievers, but God's Word tells us that believers have a reason to be joyful. We don't have to go through our lives as miserable lost souls with no reason to be hopeful and joyous.

This is another way to separate the true Christian from the merely professing type. Without the assurance of true salvation, it is impossible for people to behave in any other way than with anger, misery, and a host of other negative displays of personality. That is the way of the natural man, because it is in his nature. It is his curse, and he cannot overcome this state on his own. It is not enough just to profess he is a Christian; he will show through his behavior that he is no longer part of the norm. It will be evident to all that there is something unusual about his behavior. This is another test of our faith which can be applied from Scripture.

Another example of hypocritical behavior on the part of professing Christians is their inability to live a life of servitude towards others. Because it is so contradictory to our normal behavior pattern, we cannot willfully submit ourselves as servants. It goes against our entire make up of taking care of number one: our "self."

The opposite behavior is what our Lord actually taught us to practice. He told us He came to serve; not to be served. This is something which cannot be done by the natural man; it takes a supernaturally transformed man to fulfill this calling. Once again we find that without the help of the Holy Spirit, we will fail miserably in displaying this characteristic which should shine through in the true believer's life.

When observing this characteristic of servant hood, it will also be apparent that the objective is strictly in the service itself. That is, there is no ulterior motive of gaining acknowledgement from the act of service. Many secularists perform acts of donating time or money towards some charitable institution, but much of the time they are looking for some form of reward or honor for their involvement. This will not be the case with the true Christian; they will perform acts of servant hood just for the sake of doing so. They will not be looking to receive a reward of some kind from society.

Still another area which may give evidence to the hypocritical professor of Christianity can be the inability to simply let their yes be yes and their no be no. Today's society thinks calling a falsehood by a name such as a "white lie," somehow diminishes it to less than what it really is: a lie. If you listen to talk shows or read books on relationships, you will quickly find secularists who believe it is okay to tell lies when we decide they are appropriate for certain situations.

An example of the extent to which this has progressed in our culture was put on display by a government official when responding to questions about a sexual affair. When accused of stating a falsehood, his response was to say that his answers were "legally accurate." Failure to be able to admit to our own falsehoods, represents the magnitude to which the world has pushed this condition. This is another trait which cannot remain in a true believer as a characteristic of their life. Although it's true they will fail to tell the truth at some time, it will not be one of their defining characteristics. When they fail in this area, they will acknowledge their shortcoming and strive to correct this weakness in themselves with the help of the Holy Spirit.

These have all been characteristics which can be found in people who profess to be Christian, but when spending time with them, you notice their faith does not show through in their daily walk. They may not actively attack believers who do exhibit the qualities Scripture says should be seen in us, but it is still not too difficult to see the differences between them and the followers of Christ who really strive to live as God has commanded.

There is still one more area which almost always shows

through as a separation barrier between these two groups of hypocritical and true believers. I have saved this one for the last in this category of the "well-concealed" variety, because it is the one secular society has tried the hardest to legitimize.

Have you guessed what this next trait will be? It should not be so hard. In fact, it should be quite easy. When you watch the television, read the newspaper, look at a magazine, observe billboards, go to the theater, listen to the radio, or basically do anything else which requires the use of your eyes or ears; it is impossible not to notice the fascination this world has in the area of sex. In today's secular society, there is nothing people spend more time, money, and effort on than their sexual appetites.

There is nothing new about our pre-occupation with sex, for it has been the same way throughout our history. The difference today is in how society is trying to legitimize this obsession with sex in every way imaginable. There are countless psychologists and psychiatrists who have written books on this matter. There is an inexhaustible supply of talk shows on television to reinforce this view of sexual freedom. Magazines have written every kind of article imagined to add to this free expression of sexuality. Hollywood cannot seem to do enough in their efforts to insure sex remains the most talked about subject under the sun. The envelope is pushed harder and harder every year on the television. No time slot is "safe for family viewing" any longer, because what used to be forbidden in the "prime time" slot designated for family viewing is now virtually required on any shows airing today.

It is harder to go to a clothing store and purchase outfits which are not designed with this same agenda in mind. Parents with daughters are hard pressed to find anything for them to wear which is not made in a provocative and revealing fashion. It does not seem to matter what the age group is you are shopping for; styles are the same. Clothing is designed with sex appeal in mind, and the advertising of these styles is just as obvious in its intent. If you visit any shopping center, it is impossible not to be bombarded by these facts. You cannot deny it is so; it is a fact of our society.

It is just as hard for parents of sons, because there is the same agenda on their behalf. Clothing is advertised in the same manner for boys as for girls, and sex is the driving force behind nearly everything when it is designed. You cannot miss seeing this as fact unless you choose to bury your head in the sand. It is everywhere, it is in everything, and it is an obsession with no apparent boundaries. I hate to admit it, but I believe we have not yet seen the limits of this movement. I do not like to even imagine what the final barriers will be when society reaches its goal of the ultimate freedom of sexual expression.

Here lies the trait which I saved until last to separate the "well-concealed" variety of hypocritical Christians from those trying to live by God's laws. This sexual freedom is so abundant in our society, and it is another area we can use to discern between those who practice Christian values and those who simply profess to. It is plain to see that our society believes whole-heartedly in "anything goes," in the area of sex. Computer-generated drawings have made it possible to use images of children in sexually explicit scenes; they are only images and not live bodies, so they can slide around child pornography laws.

Our society has been stretching the parameters of accepted sexual behavior for quite some time. They really began to run with this agenda starting with the "free love" movement of the 1960's, and have continued running at a faster and faster pace ever since. Have you ever noticed the way secular magazines have all but removed the words spouse, husband, or wife from their articles dealing with couples? They have been thoughtfully replaced by words such as lover, significant other, current partner, or mate. This is just one of the subtle ways used for changing the perspective people had held for so long about what couples should be. The very institution of marriage itself has now fallen under attack through this sexual revolution, and society is determined to win this battle.

Biblical teaching on marriage had been widely accepted in virtually all the world for thousands of years. That is no longer the case thanks to the efforts of secularists in our court systems, in the media, and in our government. They are now being replaced with whatever these groups wish to use as their own standards for relationships; or more accurately, a lack of standards.

One of the most obvious agendas is to destroy the very foundation of marriage as given to us by God, which can be found in the book of Matthew 19:4–6:

> "Haven't you read," he replied, "that at the beginning the Creator 'made them male and female,' and said, "For this reason a man will leave his father and mother and be united to his wife, and the two will become one flesh?" So they are no longer two, but one. Therefore what God has joined together, let man not separate."

God stated for us from the very beginning that a marriage is between one man and one woman. Today, homosexual activists are aggressively attempting to abolish what God said on marriage from our society. Although the majority of citizens have voted to enforce the Biblical view in many states, activist judges are systematically declaring the majority view as being irrelevant. These judges have decided they alone will determine whether there is a standard or not.

This homosexual activism has pushed itself into many churches still claiming to be Christian in their belief. As time has passed, some of these churches have moved beyond casual acceptance of homosexual lifestyles, and declared them as "acceptable" behavior. Openly homosexual people have now moved into leadership roles of these denominations, and they have incorporated their own misinterpretations into what used to be an unquestionably accurate Biblical doctrine on marriage.

This is one lifestyle a professing Christian cannot be satisfied to live in, because there is no way to remove the evident hypocrisy. Scripture speaks concretely about homosexual behavior in both the Old and New Testaments. One example can be found in Leviticus 18:22; "Do not lie with a man as one lies with a woman; that is detestable." Another can be found in 1 Corinthians 6:9–10:

> Do you not know that the wicked will not inherit the kingdom of God? Do not be deceived: Neither the sexually immoral nor idolaters nor adulterers nor male prostitutes nor homosexual offenders nor thieves nor the greedy nor drunkards nor slanderers nor swindlers will inherit the kingdom of God.

Please understand that I do not mean to say no Christian will ever fall victim in this area of sexual sin; what I am saying is that our Bible says no Christian can ever *live* this way. Some Christians will most assuredly fail at some time in this area, but they will not stay in their transgressions. The true Christian will feel conviction, remorse, and will be sorry for their downfall. It is the same in all areas of sin, because this is the method God uses to bring us to the place of true repentance.

There are professing Christians who are living together as though they were married, but are not. This is also something that is so obviously non-scriptural, and yet it is rapidly turning into the accepted norm for our society. It is so widespread in its existence, that most church going people seem to dismiss any objections to it as being old-fashioned. This attitude has made it possible for couples practicing this lifestyle to feel even more justified in their choice.

Our Bibles tell us clearly to rebuke our fellow believers for this type of sinful behavior; it does not say we should accept them as brethren with no complaint. This type of offense was punishable by stoning in the days of the Old Testament, but Jesus put an end to that when dealing with the crowd chasing after an adulteress caught in the act. Most people readily accept the message He taught in dealing with this when no one could step forward when He asked for "he without sin" to cast the first stone. But we seem to conveniently forget how He still rebuked the woman, and told her to sin no more.

God's Word clearly states how we are to live in the realm of sexual experience. Man is just trying to re-write it, manipulate it, and re-invent what is written there. Man is doing this to comfort himself while doing what he knows is wrong. The Bible tells us precisely what is acceptable to God and what is not; and all Christians must accept the Bible as the infallible Word of God.

God's Word tells us the only type of sex which has His blessing is between a husband and wife. There is no other example given which He approved of. There is no approval of casual sex. There is no approval of fornication between two unmarried people just because they mutually consent to it. It is forbidden for a married person to have sex with someone they are not married to; that is adultery. God does not say it is okay if you have been married before, but are now widowed or divorced. The only type of sex to which God has given His blessing is *marital* sex; without exception. No other type of sexual encounter imaginable is acceptable to God.

I realize writing those simple facts down will irritate some who may read them, but it was God who told us what should be. Can we challenge the wisdom of the Creator? You cannot choose only certain passages from God's Word for your own personalized Christian belief system, and eliminate those which don't fit into what you want your vision of Christianity to be.

The worldly man will never follow the guidelines God has given to us. Only believers can change and have a chance to live a life according to God's plan, and only when they have the Holy Spirit leading them. Again, there will always be some believers who will fall into different areas of sexual sin, but only false believers will stay in their transgressions and live a life of sexual sin. True believers will be convicted of their sinful behavior, they will confess their sins, they will be lead to repentance, and they will overcome through the strength of their relationship with Christ.

If you have let yourself be convinced you don't need a relationship with God because of professing believers you have known who are habitually involved in any of these types of sexual behaviors; you have been duped. I do not mean any Christian you are aware of who has fallen at one time or another, but then has risen and overcome the transgression. I am warning about the ones who profess to be believers, but they live a sexual lifestyle that is directly contradictory to what God's Word says.

It is impossible not to notice that our world has given its stamp of approval to practically every type of sexual activity man has dreamed up. Our legal systems endorse them, Hollywood makes movies highlighting them, our educators teach our children they are acceptable, and the magazine industry glorifies the sexual lifestyles people practice.
Although these types of sexual immorality are so easy to observe, they are probably the most overlooked sinful activities of all. They can be hard to see, because the world has told us for so long that there is nothing wrong with these types of sexual behaviors. The words adultery and fornication are almost absent from our vocabulary; they have been replaced by words like affair or indiscretion. Adultery and fornication are too much like Biblical words for our society, it reminds people of God. People don't want to be reminded of God when they are guilty of this type of behavior.

Please, make sure if you find yourself involved in one of these types of activities, that you are aware of the fact that God has placed them all under the heading of sexual immorality. A true believer will not participate in any of them as a deliberate and intentional choice for a lifestyle. You will be convicted and repentant. You will stop falling into this area of sin, because you know it is offending your God. You may fall for a time; but you will always get back up.

3rd Layer:
The Almost Impossible to Recognize Hypocrite

Now let's look at the deepest layer of hypocritical believer, the layer I call the "almost impossible to recognize" variety.

These are people who call themselves Christian with much vigor and confidence. They may exhibit many of the same traits I have listed in the previous two layers, but it may be much more difficult to discover the evidence of these characteristics in them. In fact, you may never discover the contradictions in their lives unless they choose to inform you of them.

The reason I label this group as being "almost impossible to recognize," is because they have a characteristic in them, which makes it so. The common thread running throughout this layer lies in the fact that they tend to believe wholeheartedly in their salvation. I do not mean to say they merely profess their belief with their mouths; I mean in their hearts and minds they are convinced of their salvation. It is this deeply felt belief, which makes it so difficult to reach them. Unless you develop a deep and meaningful relationship with someone in this category, you will most likely never even realize the turmoil present underneath his or her confident exterior. On top of that, as I stated just prior; even then you will probably not be aware of their condition unless they choose to share it with you.

Our accuser, who is called satan or the devil, will work non-stop to place doubts and turmoil into the hearts of the most devout believers of our faith. He is able to cast doubt into all of us from time to time. It may be in our questioning the reasons why events occur in our lives such as illnesses, hardships, the passing of loved ones, and other such trials and tribulations we must endure. The blessed fact for the true believer lies in the Holy Spirit's presence to help us as we travel through those times in our lives. The horrible reality is that He is not there for the false believer. I have only been told by a few fellow believers of different times when they have come into contact with a person who falls into this category. I am not sure whether this group is so rare that we scarcely become aware of any instances, or if it is in the difficulty of uncovering their condition which makes it so rare.

The factors leading to the beliefs these individuals hold, and the extreme difficulty in overcoming them, are what we are going to be looking at. These deeply held principles are not developed over night; they are part of a system of ideals which have been built up over a long period of time. They will be cemented into the very foundation of this person's identity. So if you are ever given the privilege of mentoring this type of individual, please understand that it will be no small undertaking.

You will be tested in your own strength. If you ever find yourself taking on this type of challenge, satan will put great effort into trying to shake your own foundation. You will need much prayer, and you will need to spend a great amount of time in God's Word. Through it all, you must remember it is only through the grace of God that victory will ever be achieved.

One of the most misunderstood parts of the Bible deals with the doctrinal belief that once a believer has been forgiven and saved, they are always saved. There is a small minority of professing Christians who do not believe this doctrine to be true; but I am not one of them. I believe once we have truly attained our salvation we shall never lose it; the key is whether our belief is genuine or not.

The problem does not lie in the doctrine itself; the problem is in how we go about determining if we have truly received the gift of salvation. The Apostle Paul states very plainly how to receive our salvation in Romans 10: 9–10; "That if you confess with your mouth, 'Jesus is Lord,' and believe in your heart that God raised him from the dead, you will be saved. For it is with your heart that you believe and are justified, and it is with your mouth that you confess and are saved."

Pay careful attention to Paul's statement that we must believe with our hearts in God's raising Jesus Christ from the grave, in order to be saved. He says, "It is with your heart that you believe and are justified." Then we will profess our belief with our mouths; and be saved. We need to understand this doctrine shows us a two-part process we will complete before we receive this salvation.

One way we can go astray in this doctrine, is in our thinking that we must have believed in our heart in order to have been able to confess with our lips that Jesus is Lord. This way of thinking can create a false sense of having done everything required to receive our salvation. This false sense of security convinces us that we are safe in the arms of the Lord. The longer we live this way, the more sure we become of ourselves.

The real difficulty lies in the concept of believing. We easily confess with our mouth that Jesus is Lord, but believing in the heart is where we have the most difficulty. We must take the time and make the effort necessary to know that when we have confessed with our mouths; first we have truly believed with our hearts. It is not enough to probably believe, or maybe to believe, or think we believe, or even want to believe; we must truly believe! To help you understand what I mean by "truly," I will refer to the Webster's Dictionary once again. Webster's says it means the concept of total sincerity in an agreement of something as fact, without feigning, falsity, or possible inaccuracy in one's position; this is how we must believe in our hearts!

This is the most common reason for someone to fall into this category I label the "almost impossible to recognize" variety. It has nothing to do with them not wanting to be true believers; they sincerely do. Their salvation means more to them than anything else in their lives. They desire their salvation with all of their heart. When they heard the Gospel message, they wanted to believe with all of their heart. The sad reality is that sometimes we can convince ourselves we have believed, when in truth; we have not really done so. There is such a fine line between this wanting to believe and truly believing; but the fact is this line does exist.

This is a difficult trait to illustrate, but our Lord did so in Matthew 13: 3–8 and 18–23:

> Then he told them many things in parables, saying: "A farmer went out to sow his seed. As he was scattering the seed, some fell along the path, and the birds came and ate it up. Some fell on rocky places, where it did not have much soil. It sprang up quickly, because the soil was shallow. But when the sun came up, the plants were scorched, and they withered because they had no root. Other seed fell among thorns, which grew up and choked the plants. Still other seed fell on good soil, where it produced a crop—a hundred, sixty or thirty times what was sown."
>
> "Listen then to what the parable of the sower means: When anyone hears the message about the kingdom and does not understand it, the evil one comes and snatches away what was sown in his heart. This is the seed sown along the path. The one who received the seed that fell on rocky places is the man who hears the word and at once receives it with joy. But since he has no root, he lasts only a short time. When trouble

or persecution comes because of the word, he quickly falls away. The one who received the seed that fell among the thorns is the man who hears the word, but the worries of this life and the deceitfulness of wealth choke it, making it unfruitful. But the one who received the seed that fell on good soil is the man who hears the word and understands it. He produces a crop, yielding a hundred, sixty or thirty times what was sown."

I believe this "almost impossible to recognize" variety are the ones on the rocky soil who receive the Word with joy when they hear it, but have no root. They believe for a while, but then fall away. This type of belief is only superficial, and it does not save them. They may have only been "caught up in the moment" during an emotional church service, and thought it made great sense to be a Christian. However, their heart may not have been truly involved in their thinking this way, so true repentance never took place. I know it can be hard to understand, but to sum it up; *it* **does not matter how sincerely you believe in your own belief, if your belief is not truly sincere to begin with**.

As with the previous two varieties of hypocritical believers, the Sermon on the Mount should be used to examine the validity of their claims. It is infallible, as all Scripture is. If proof of faith is not found in their walk, urge them to re-examine whether they truly believe in Christ or not. If you feel you may fall into this category, I urge you to enlist the aid of your pastor, a Christian counselor, or someone you feel is a true brother or sister in your church. Seek God through prayer, fasting, and searching the Scripture. Ask the Holy Spirit to speak to you, He will do so. Our Father in Heaven desires for us to be with Him, He will not forsake you; ask

Him to help you with your unbelief.

These are the three types of hypocritical Christians I have encountered in my walk. Some of them may be easily observed, some may be very difficult to notice, and still others may be nearly impossible to notice. Reality lies in the fact these hypocritical professors of the Christian faith are present in our world.

There are so many non-believers using this excuse of hypocrisy for their own failure to accept God's gift of salvation, its existence cannot be disputed. It is the true believers who must strive to let Christ show through their walk so non-believers and false believers alike will see the differences in them, and be drawn to discover why these differences are there. Then, they also may believe on the Lord and become truly saved, and become positive witnesses for others, instead of negative ones.

Chapter Two

You Can't *Prove* It

When I was a young man, I became a journeyman Tool & Die maker after serving an apprenticeship in a small job shop. I have worked for almost thirty years now in this field, and I have been able to witness to many of my co-workers along the way. I have also been fortunate enough to have co-workers that helped my faith mature by sharing with me. Part of the motivation for this chapter comes from the comments that one particular co-worker made to me during a lunch break discussion, which have served as the title for this chapter, "You can't prove it."

This comment is one that I have heard from many others that I have talked with, or at least something very similar to it. At the time that my friend said this, he was using it to finish off his defense on why he never "fell" for the whole "religious" thing. He was nice enough in the way that he went about it, but he made his feelings plain. He told me that I was the kind of guy that he couldn't quite figure out because I seemed "too smart" to fall for all that "religious" stuff. He was referring to my ability to lead a job crew and to think through the job at hand because those were the types of skills that he believed need intelligence to complete.

This whole concept of "falling" for Christianity is what this chapter is going to deal with, and the agenda behind it. I know it's something that we have all heard at one time or another because so many people use this excuse that it ranks right behind hypocrisy. It serves as a way to make people feel better about denying Christ if they can say it's because they're too smart to be "taken in by religion," but the real issue is: *are they being "taken in by something else*?"

There's nothing new about this argument. Men were using it when Jesus was walking on this Earth, and they are still using it today. The question has always been asked since it arose in the very beginning; Is man smart enough not to need God? We can read in Genesis 3:1–13:

> Now the serpent was more crafty than any of the wild animals the Lord God had made. He said to the woman, "Did God really say, 'You must not eat fruit from any tree in the garden'?"
>
> The woman said to the serpent, "We may eat fruit from the trees in the garden, but God did say, 'You must not eat fruit from the tree that is in the middle of the garden, and you must not touch it, or you will die.'"
>
> "You will not surely die," the serpent said to the woman. "For God knows that when you eat of it your eyes will be opened, and you will be like God, knowing

good and evil."

When the woman saw that the fruit of the tree was good for food and pleasing to the eye, and also desirable for gaining wisdom, she took some and ate it. She also gave some to her husband, who was with her, and he ate it. Then the eyes of both of them were opened, and they realized they were naked; so they sewed fig leaves together and made coverings for themselves.

Then the man and his wife heard the sound of the Lord God as he was walking in the garden in the cool of the day, and they hid from the Lord God among the trees of the garden. But the Lord God called to the man, "Where are you?"

He answered, "I heard you in the garden, and I was afraid because I was naked; so I hid."

And He said, "Who told you that you were naked? Have you eaten from the tree that I commanded you not to eat from?"

The man said, "The woman you put here with me--she gave me some fruit from the tree, and I ate it."

Then the Lord God said to the woman, "What is this you have done?" The woman said, "The serpent deceived me, and I ate."

So we see men have wanted to be as smart as God since the beginning, and that made it easy for the serpent to "trick" us into eating from the forbidden tree. It wasn't just because the "forbidden" fruit looked like it would taste good; it was also desirable for gaining wisdom. Ever since, this has been one of the devil's most used schemes—keeping us believing that we are smart enough that we don't need God. It's really not that hard for this trick to keep working since pride has a way of making us want to see ourselves being as wise as God.

When I read that passage, I can't help but notice another trait that is so common among men: how incapable we are of accepting responsibility for our actions when they get us into trouble. When God asked the man if he ate the forbidden fruit, did you see how quickly he blamed the woman for giving it to him and God for giving him the woman? Then, the woman joined the show by blaming the serpent for her downfall, completing their own little pity party. I see this as our first example of how man reacts when he realizes he has made a mistake; excuses were born.

Isn't it a shame that the first thing man's new wisdom was used for was to excuse his own wrongdoing in gaining it? That was the beginning of our making excuses, and it hasn't stopped yet. People are inventing new ones to fit every little thing we do that we know is wrong, but don't want to admit. The world has placed the highest value on knowledge and made it one of the most sought after possessions men can have. But we are going to see, there is a big difference between the knowledge men seek at secular colleges, and wisdom that comes from God.

Students in our colleges are taught in a way that defines how things are and what makes them as they are. In mathematics and science, you are taught about certain "laws" that can't be broken; they have been "proven." It is the same for virtually every field that men study in what we call "higher education," so I won't get bogged down trying to hit on each one specifically. The theme running through our education system deals with man's figuring out the things in our world that "repeat" over time, and then we call them "proofs" or "laws of nature." Whenever someone figures out that one of these "laws" wasn't quite right it is called a breakthrough discovery and the "new truth." One of the things that amazes me about this is how they don't acknowledge the fact of being wrong in their original understanding, or how their latest "truth" is only good as long as it is not also discovered to be wrong by someone else later on.

Another thing I have noticed about the secular education system is how it puts the most emphasis on the "physical" parts of our universe. By that, I mean the things we can put our "hands on" to touch, feel, and see around us. I think this is because men have been able to observe the physical world God created, and they feel confident in what I call man's ability to "have a firm grasp of the obvious." We have to admit that men have done a very good job of figuring out how things work in our world, in our bodies, and in our universe; where they lack is in understanding the reasons things work as they do. I believe the reason for this is because in order to understand that part of our world, you must move out of the physical realm and into the spiritual one; but they place no value on the spiritual world because they can't see it (in more ways than one).

What God brings to man is wisdom, which Webster's defines as the power of true and right discernment, and the actions that are dictated by such discernment. God isn't going to be pleased by how much stuff we know, but He is pleased when we put what we know to good use. This is what we need to focus our energy on; using our knowledge to accomplish what God has planned for our life rather than on how much knowledge we can obtain. It is so easy to get caught up in how many different "degrees" you can acquire from universities, and to lose sight of what you planned to do with the learning in the first place.

Men found themselves getting "caught up" in this same kind of trouble during the time when Jesus was here on earth, so it's nothing new. An amazing thing is how higher education is able to "see" the way things work and fit together in our universe, but is unable to recognize the fact that someone set things in place that way to begin with, namely, God. The fact that these secular scholar-types can believe that the universe somehow all came to fit together perfectly through chance is something that I could never understand if it wasn't for the Scriptures found in God's Word.

There are many passages that will help us to understand this condition, such as 1 Corinthians 1:19–21,25:

> For it is written: I will destroy the wisdom of the wise; the intelligence of the intelligent I will frustrate." Where is the wise man? Where is the scholar? Where is the philosopher of this age? Has not God made foolish the wisdom of this world? For since in the wisdom of God the world through its wisdom did not know him, God was pleased through the foolishness of what was preached to save those who believe. For the foolishness of God is wiser than man's wisdom, and the weakness of God is stronger than man's strength.

Another passage that we can turn to is 1 Corinthians 3:18–20;

> Do not deceive yourselves. If any one of you thinks he is wise by the standards of this age, he should become a 'fool' so that he may become wise. For the wisdom of this world is foolishness in God's sight. As it is written: "He catches the wise in their craftiness', and again, 'The Lord knows that the thoughts of the wise are futile."

Taken together, these passages give us a clear warning: we're a lot better off to look for God's wisdom than for what the world calls intelligence. If you are counting on the knowledge of this world to take care of your troubles, then you have forsaken God. We are told about this condition in Psalm 14:1–3:

> The fool says in his heart, 'There is no God.' They are corrupt, their deeds are vile; there is no one who does good. The Lord looks down from heaven on the sons of men to see if there are any who understand, any who seek God. All have turned aside, they have together become corrupt; there is no one who does good, not even one.

Not a very pretty picture of man's state, but an accurate one.

So we see that the intelligence of the world is useless if you don't apply the wisdom of God to it. However, if you don't acknowledge God's existence, you obviously can't apply His wisdom. Now, just in case you might be thinking that I am saying we who believe in God are way ahead of everyone who doesn't believe, I want to share another passage with you from James 2:19; "You believe that there is one God. Good! Even the demons believe that—and shudder." So don't get all excited just because you believe in God. As we have already read it is the fool who says in his heart that there is no God.

People have grown convinced that if they can't see, smell, touch, or taste something; it doesn't exist. If you can't physically present it for examination, then it must not be real in the first place. So it is our physical senses that are used to determine whether or not something is legitimate, thus eliminating everything spiritual in one giant swing. This is why so many people practice atheism through living a life that denies God's existence.

There are many examples we can use to challenge this need for physical proof. One of them would be to ask a person whether or not he or she believes in the existence of love. Do you believe that your mother loved you? Do you love your mother? If you are married, have you loved your spouse? These are just a couple examples of the condition that we call love, but they can prove the point. When we are honest, we must admit that at one time or another we have known that love does exist. But we must also admit that we can't prove it. Love is there because we feel it in our hearts, but we can't pull it out and set it down for observation. That doesn't make it any less real though, does it?

One of my favorite examples to use is the existence of good and evil. You can't put either of them into a test tube to examine, but does anyone want to deny that they exist? Right and wrong, good and bad: these are two of the basic building blocks of our behavior that we must have in order to live together. They are not something that you can pull out and look at, but everyone knows that they exist. I wish it wasn't so, but I find that evil is the easiest of the two to use as an example. If we are honest, we all have to admit that we see "wrongs" happening all around us. I wish that we could as easily see examples in which "right" was the dominating force, but experience shows it is not.

There are many more examples we could look at, but these two serve the purpose. There are many things in our life that we know exist, but we can't physically prove them. So why does anyone say that God doesn't exist because He can't be physically proven? The same argument won't hold up when used against things like love or right and wrong, so why is God any different? When it comes to knowing that love is real, where do we find that proof? It's through the heart that we know love is real, and God uses the same method to show us that He is real, too.

We read in Romans 10:10; "For it is with your heart that you believe and are justified, and it is with your mouth that you confess and are saved." And another passage is Psalm 37:30–31; "The mouth of the righteous man utters wisdom, and his tongue speaks what is just. The law of his God is in his heart: his feet do not slip." These passages tell us that it is with our hearts that we will believe in God, and it is also where God lays His laws of right and wrong. So if we choose to ignore or dismiss the feelings that come to us through our hearts, we will never come to know God.

So Scripture tells us that we will believe in God through our hearts, but it also says that our mind must become convinced. One of the places that this is found is in Mark 12: 28–30; "One of the teachers of the law came and heard them debating. Noticing that Jesus had given them a good answer, he asked him, 'Of all the commandments, which is the most important?' 'The most important one,' answered Jesus, 'is this: Hear O Israel, the Lord our God, the Lord is one. Love the Lord your God with all your heart and with all your soul and with all your mind and with all your strength.'"

We are to love God with our hearts and with our minds as well. Then we are to show our love with all of our strength by putting our love into action through our deeds. So we will first feel God in our hearts, then we can be convinced in our minds through His Word, and finish it off through serving Him with our deeds. It is with heart, mind, and the exercising of our will through serving Him that will show others that God is real in our lives. I have found that seeing this type of example in those around me is the closest thing to physical proof that I can find for God's existence. When you know someone who has truly become a Christian, you can see the difference that God makes in his or her life. If you are an analytical person who demands proof in order to believe something, this is probably the closest you will come to it.

So in closing out this chapter on the problem of not being able to prove God's existence, I hope it has helped you. I can't offer you physical proof of God any more than I can show you physical proof of love or good and evil. But, we all know that these exist, and we can all point out examples of them from our lives. So I urge you not to shut God out just because you can't touch Him. You wouldn't deny love in your life because you can't touch it. Love is real and so is God. He has placed His laws on your heart, and that is why you know the difference between right and wrong. Man has been trying to deny that fact since he was created, but it keeps proving itself with each newborn that comes along.

If you find yourself using the lack of physical evidence as an excuse for denying God and His plan of salvation, I beg you to listen to your heart. When you feel love for someone, do you question whether it physically exists? When you know the difference between right and wrong, do you question how you know it or do you just accept it as truth? These are the closest types of proofs that we can offer, but if you will let your heart help you to decide, they will be more than enough! God is real, and it doesn't matter that I can't point Him out to you. It doesn't matter that we can't reach out and touch Him, any more than we can touch love; but we know it is there.

Ask God to touch your heart and soften it so that the hardness that comes from this world won't interfere with your sense of feeling His presence. If you let Him speak to you in that way, He will fill you with such a sense of knowing He is there that you will no longer need physical proof to believe it. He will enter your heart and change your life in a way that will help others to see the reality of His existence. You will become part of the proof that others need to see in order to believe, and that is the best thing that we can find ourselves a part of. You will find yourself in the position that all believers are in: knowing in their hearts that they have been saved but unable to physically prove it. However, I guarantee you that this won't be a problem for you as a believer, because the overwhelming knowledge that Jesus Christ has entered your heart, mind, and soul will reassure you every day for the rest of your life.

Chapter Three

I Can't Afford the Price Tag

Following Christ is a choice and it comes with a price. The price tag reads, "The Ultimate Price." The price is your life. Why not go ahead and make the decision to follow Christ? Is that price on the tag overwhelmingly high? Can you bring yourself to write that spiritual check? This cost is many things to different individuals. For some it is the financial cost, or you might not want to risk the possible embarrassment. Perhaps you simply don't want to give up many of the things you like to do. Are you worried that a life with Christ will add to your already full "to do" list? There are many issues that come to mind when people feel the "sticker shock" after viewing this ultimate price tag. Let's take a look at a few of the most common issues.

***Prices* Listed on the Tags:**

Price Tag #1: Money

Is there a financial cost of taking up one's cross and following Jesus? Of course. Two obvious areas of financial commitment are tithes and offerings. Churches need these from their congregations in order to function. This is the most obvious place to start, as we are all aware of the fact that churches pass an offering plate during their services for the purpose of collecting the money needed to run the church and its ministries.

The Word of God states very precisely that God has ordained for us to give Him one-tenth of our earnings. This is stated in the book of Leviticus 27:30–32:

> A tithe of everything from the land, whether grain from the soil or fruit from the trees, belongs to the Lord; it is holy to the Lord. If a man redeems any of his tithe, he must add a fifth of the value to it. The entire tithe of the herd and flock—every tenth animal that passes under the shepherd's rod—will be holy to the Lord.

Here, Moses passed down the law as it was given to him by God. God's Word also says in the book of Genesis 28:20–22:

> Then Jacob made a vow saying, "If God will be with me and will watch over me on this journey I am taking and will give me food to eat and clothes to wear so that I return safely to my father's house, then the Lord will be my God and this stone that I have set up as a pillar will be God's house, and of all that you give me I will give you a tenth."

There are many other references which place the value to be offered at one-tenth of one's earnings, but it's usually not the percentage people complain about so much as it is the act of giving itself.

In the New Testament, there are also many references made on this subject of giving. We read in 2 Corinthians 9:6–8: "Remember this: Whoever sows sparingly will also reap sparingly, and whoever sows generously will also reap generously. Each man should give what he has decided in his heart to give, not reluctantly or under compulsion, for God loves a cheerful giver."

This same thought is echoed again in Luke 6:38; "Give and it will be given to you. A good measure, pressed down, shaken together and running over, will be poured in your lap. For with the measure you use, it will be measured to you." In the book of Acts 20:35, we are told by Jesus; "It is more blessed to give than it is to receive." Also in 1 Corinthians 16:1–2, the Apostle Paul tells us, "Now about the collection for God's people: do what I told the Galatian churches to do. On the first day of every week, each one of you should set aside a sum of money in keeping with his income, saving it up, so that when I come no collection will have to be made."

In the Old Testament book of Proverbs 11:24, God's Word states; "One man gives freely, yet gains even more; another withholds unduly, but comes to poverty." And in Proverbs 28:27; "He who gives to the poor will lack nothing while he who closes his eyes to them receives many curses." These are more promises from God that He will place His blessings on those that give as He has asked of them. Our Bible is full of these promises, and warnings.

So, can you see it was not the church that created this concept of tithing, but instead it was God Himself who ordained it? It was for the ability of His church to function that God commanded our offerings to be given. We must understand our tithes and offerings are a holy sacrifice we make to our God, not to our churches. Wherever you attend and present your offering, it is simply the vessel through which God is working.

Have you or someone you know ever complained about this concept of tithing? You'll notice that the root of most complaints stem from a lack of understanding. The church merely organizes our offerings in order to serve God's kingdom the best way possible. Giving our tithes and offerings unto God is an act of worship, and an example of our obedience to His Word. However, He does not call for our blind obedience in tithing, and it is only common sense for us to make sure our offerings are being used to further God's kingdom wherever we present them. If we can come to understand the true concept of tithing, we can eliminate the question "What are they doing with my money?" Just remember: everything really belongs to God to begin with.

Before I became a born-again believer, this was one of the hang-ups I had in my own life. One of the reasons I had a problem with the financial cost of making an offering at church was because I still had a worldview of life. My parents raised me under the notion of needing a higher education in order to earn as much money as I possibly could once I joined the workforce. I ended up going the route of working in a skilled trade's job instead of college, following in the footsteps of my father. Actually, he helped me enter into my apprenticeship in the Tool & Die trade. He told me that if I was not going to go on in college, this would be the next best option as far as earning potential was concerned. He was right, as I have always been gainfully employed, and indeed I am still working in a related field to this day.

Focusing on the importance of earning as much money as possible in life caused me to place a value on money that proved hard to overcome. I fell into the classic trap of trying to "keep up with the Jones." I developed an overwhelming desire to accumulate as many worldly possessions as I possibly could. The problem isn't in the money itself, but in our love for it. God's Word says in 1 Timothy 6:10; "For the love of money is a root of all kinds of evil. Some people, eager for money, have wandered from the faith and pierced themselves with many griefs." It is how we feel about money in our hearts causing us harm when we place its value ahead of all others. Money itself is nothing more than a necessary tool of life, and we need the provisions it supplies to keep the ministries we are called to support alive.

It's not hard to understand how this type of attitude causes us to have such a difficult time accepting godly principles on tithing. I was trying to earn as much as possible, and to acquire treasures accordingly. That kind of living makes no allowances for giving money away, and getting nothing of measure in return. I tried for years to overcome it while attending church regularly. I always managed to give some amount, but never the tenth God had established as His standard. I tried to reason with God, trying to convince myself that if I was content with the amount I gave, I qualified as a cheerful giver. This meant, in weeks I didn't feel like it, I simply didn't give because God wouldn't be pleased with it.

Looking back now, I am amazed by how easily I was able to reconcile myself to this philosophy. I can see where satan was able to slip right into my mind, and easily manipulate my thought process on this matter. Using the world-instilled value system, it was no challenge for him to trick me into believing that I was doing the right thing. How foolish we are with ourselves, falling victim to our own beliefs. Christians just need to follow the commands God gave us in His Word. We have to realize we are still living by the standards of the world when we are not willing to tithe as God commanded; it's that simple.

God's Word says in Matthew 6:24; "No one can serve two masters. Either he will hate the one and love the other, or he will be devoted to the one and despise the other. You cannot serve both God and Money." The truth contained in this verse, "You cannot love both God and money," cannot be overemphasized. Yet, even though I had read it many times, I was still able to dismiss this truth from my own mind. I fell victim, like so many others, to the notion of not seeing myself as being guilty of this horrible sin of loving money. That is the problem with living in the worldview instead of the Christian one: we are blind to our own sins.

If you are using the financial excuse as one of the reasons for not accepting Christianity as your personal lifestyle, I want to share some passages from God's Word warning against this very thing. It's not like this is something new to modern man, we have been in love with our money and possessions from the beginning. In Mark 8:36 we are asked by Jesus; "What good is it for a man to gain the whole world, yet forfeit his soul?" The meaning of this verse is plainly stated, and yet again we can ignore the warning stated there. Remember what we read in 1 Timothy 6:10; "For the love of money is a root of all kinds of evil. Some people, eager for money, have wandered from the faith and pierced themselves with many griefs." I believe almost everybody has heard this saying, and yet it is easy to ignore if you are still living in the set ways of the world.

In the Old Testament, Solomon taught us in the book of

Ecclesiastes 5:10; "Whoever loves money never has money enough; whoever loves wealth is never satisfied with his income. This too is meaningless." God's Word is full of warnings dealing with this love of money; all we have to do is believe what we read. We are told of the dangers involved and the consequences we will face for failing. But, we are also told the promises of the blessings we will reap if we overcome the world and live the Christian life.

One of these promises can be found in Proverbs 11:24; "One man gives freely, yet gains even more; another withholds unduly, but comes to poverty." Another promise is found in Luke 6:38; "Give, and it will be given to you. A good measure, pressed down, and shaken together and running over, will be poured into your lap. For with the measure you use, it will be measured to you." God's Word is full of these types of promises, and we can enjoy them if we will just believe and obey His commands.

There lies the root of this problem with financial misgivings; determining what it is we truly need. If you want to call yourself a Christian, but you have trouble submitting to the tithing principle as it is clearly stated in God's Word, I suggest you need to step back and look deeply at yourself. If you find yourself prone to making up your own excuses for why it's okay not to give to your church as we are told, then you need to reflect on why that is. Maybe it's because the world is still clouding your thinking.

When we submit to the will of God, we undergo a true re-birth. Everything about us changes, the old is cast out and replaced with a new creation. We finally understand how everything under the sun comes from God to begin with. It is all His, there is nothing here but by His will. Only a true believer will ever receive this understanding. If this is the case, you will not only tithe, but do so with much joy. This is from having received the revelation of the Christian life. If you are truly saved, you will have this understanding. If you find yourself in denial of this truth, you are in a dangerous position if you call yourself a Christian.

The world will cloud our vision in every way possible. That is how satan runs his kingdom. We receive this worldview at birth. It is the view of the natural man that it is natural to love your wealth. This is our original nature in regards to our finances; however, it is a sinful nature. The Christian nature makes no sense to the natural man. It goes against everything he has been taught by the world. If you find yourself thinking like the natural man when it comes to tithing, consider yourself warned by the Scriptures. You will receive God's revelation to overcome this hang-up once you truly believe, and you will become a joyful giver unto the Lord.

There is a difference between what we call tithing and what the world calls donating or charity. I am aware of many natural-minded people who are willing to donate part of their possessions to those less fortunate than they are. This is an act of noble character, and we should all be helping in this way. But, it should not be confused with giving back to God His tenth of our earnings. We are merely giving back what was already His to begin with. The worldly man may donate with the purpose of gaining admiration from others. However, we are told to avoid giving in a prideful manner in Matthew 6:3–4; "But when you give to the needy, do not let your left hand know what your right hand is doing, so that your giving may be in secret. Then your Father, who sees what is done in secret, will reward you."

This is another difference we can clearly see between the worldly man and the Christian one. If you find yourself desiring to let others know what you are giving to your church or other ministries, you are like the man who wants recognition for donating to his chosen cause or organization. If you desire accolades from others who hear of your generosity, then again you need to take a step back and reflect. This desire is a worldly one; it is not what a believer will desire. Matthew 6:1–2 warns against this type of behavior:

> Be careful not to do your acts of righteousness before men, to be seen by them. If you do, you will have no reward from your Father in heaven. So when you give to the needy, do not announce it with trumpets, as the hypocrites do in the synagogues and on the streets, to be honored by men. I tell you the truth, they have received their reward in full.

True believers will not be concerned with letting others know about their giving, they will give in secret so only the Lord knows what it is they are doing. We are told this will lead to receiving rewards in Heaven when our time on earth is through. Our perception needs to change so we will realize everything we have comes from God, not just one-tenth of it. Our use of time is the same because God doesn't ask us for just one day a week to be dedicated to Him; He asks for all seven of them.

Price tag #2: God's Demands

Now let's discuss Biblical legalistic understanding. There is a "Shalt and Shalt Not" dismissal which is definitely a common excuse not to give one's life to Christ.

When's the last time you asked God why He was so demanding? This is such a commonly asked question because so many of us think He sits on His throne looking down, commanding what we shall or shall not do. If you ask someone what they know about God, assuming they believe in Him, one trait they usually mention deals with His lording over us. Few can quote the Ten Commandments, but most have at least heard of them due to this legalistic way of thinking. Even if it is only through Hollywood's version using Charlton Heston as Moses, most people have some idea of what the Ten Commandments are. Most believe they are a list of things which God has told us we cannot do.

In our country today, we are familiar with the Ten Commandments since they are mentioned in the news almost daily. One group or another is challenging the legality of their existence in practically every state of the union. Emblems, placards, and statues that have been on display for years, are now being challenged in hope of removing them from the public arena. Secular society is using every power it has to win, and there is nothing off limits in the attacks. The goal is to remove God from public life; to strike His name from our Pledge of Allegiance, our currency, our schools, or anywhere else He is found.

The Ten Commandments are being challenged in the same way that Christianity, the Bible, and God Himself are. Man is trying to remove God from any governmental or public arenas. It is an assault gaining momentum, and the world is winning the war. Activist judges continue to make rulings removing what has been in place since the founding of our nation. This trend is one of the most troubling to Christianity in my generation. I hope the enormous amount of attention these attacks draw will cause more people to pay attention, so they can see what's really going on. I pray some will see through the secular smoke screen and recognize the true significance of God. Then they might understand why so much energy is being spent to remove Him from public life.

The Ten Commandments from God's Word are found in the book of Exodus 20:1–17. I will include a little of my own understanding of these commandments as I list them. Please read them for yourself and ask God to give you understanding as you do. As in all things, prayer first is the way to go.

The first commandment starts out with God simply stating He is God, and we are to have no other gods but Him. This is because we should recognize Him for what He is: the Holy One who was, is, and always will be. This means we shouldn't place anything ahead of God, like putting fear where faith should be. When we do, we place our belief in the enemy's message instead of the one God has given to us.

The second commandment follows the first in a common sense way; it is the command not to make or worship any form of idols. This means we should not honor anything in our lives (except for God) to the point we are actually worshipping them. By this, I don't mean we have to be physically bowing down before them, I mean we can place such value on them, in our own hearts, that it becomes a type of worship. It could be your spouse, your children or grandchildren, your career, your home, or your church: anything taking the place of where God should be in your heart.

The third commandment says we are not to take the name of God in vain. This does not only mean we should not curse using His name as is so commonly done; it really means we should not utter His name except when we are worshipping Him in prayer, praising Him, or in other ways of glorifying Him. We should always have reverence for Him when mentioning His name, even when calling ourselves Christians.

The fourth commandment is the command to remember the Sabbath day and keep it Holy. God tells us He labored for six days during Creation, and on the seventh day He rested from His labors. This is a day in which we are to rest and remember God as we worship Him.

In the fifth commandment, we are told to honor our fathers and mothers so we may live a long life. Society is attacking this commandment by tearing down the foundations of marriage and the husband/wife relationship as ordained by God. Everyone has parents, and God says to honor them because they are your parents—period.

The sixth commandment says we are not to commit murder. This commandment can be hard to understand if you don't see the difference between murdering someone and a justifiable taking of a life. God did not say never to take a life, but He did say not to murder. There are many examples in God's Word showing us where taking a life can be justified; murder was the type of killing God was forbidding in this commandment.

The seventh commandment says we shall not commit adultery. This one is easily understood; there are to be no sexual relationships of any kind whatsoever between individuals who are not married to each other. This means if you are single, you do not qualify for sexual relations. You are to wait for your marriage to take place. If you are married, then your spouse is the only person with whom you are to have sexual relations. Our society has turned sex into something as common as eating and sleeping, but society cannot change God's Word, only choose to ignore it. It doesn't matter if society is removing every negative consequence for breaking this commandment from public life. God's laws are eternal and He will punish those who break them.

The eighth commandment says we shall not steal; another one easily understood. Don't take anything from your fellow man that God has given to them, unless it is from mutual consent. We are not to make dishonest gains; all things should be acquired through honest means. Everyone knows what stealing is, and God commands us not to steal.

The ninth commandment says we are not to give false testimony; which means not to tell lies. This also means we should not deliberately say things against each other for the purpose of defaming character. God says to speak the truth in all things, so we shouldn't tell lies instead.

The tenth and final commandment says we are not to covet anything that is our neighbor's. This means to desire having something of your neighbors that doesn't belong to you. It goes beyond "keeping up with the Jones'." It means wanting to take the very possessions of the Jones', including even Mrs. Jones! It is an inward desire leading to evil intentions, and worse yet, evil doings if left unchecked.

Those are the Ten Commandments God gave to Moses, and He wrote them down in the book of Exodus. They have served as the basic building blocks of modern society. Much of our laws have been written using God's standards of justice as given in these commandments, whether society wants to admit it or not doesn't make it any less the truth.

Jesus Christ tells us in Matthew 5:17–19:

> Do not think that I have come to abolish the Law or the Prophets; I have not come to abolish them but to fulfill them. I tell you the truth, until heaven and earth disappear, not the smallest letter, not the least

> stroke of a pen, will by any means disappear from the Law until everything is accomplished. Anyone who breaks one of the least of these commandments and teaches others to do the same will be called least in the kingdom of heaven, but whoever practices and teaches these commands will be called great in the kingdom of heaven.

He also made sure we understood the law did not only deal with things we could do with our hands. He tells us "thou shalt not murder" goes beyond the physical, and we can murder someone in our hearts when we become angry with them. He tells us "thou shalt not commit adultery" is the same. We can simply look on another with lust in our hearts, and be just as guilty of breaking this commandment as if we had broken it physically.

Christ did not come to tell us we no longer have to live under these commandments. He came to fulfill them. He explained their meaning so we could all understand them. God's Word tells us in Ephesians 2:8–10; "For it is by grace you have been saved, through faith—and this not from yourselves, it is the gift of God—not by works, so that no one can boast. For we are God's workmanship, created in Christ Jesus to do good works, which God prepared in advance for us to do." However, to say we are not supposed to live by God's Law because we are now under His grace is a denial of Christ's interpreting them for us.

For the people who claim these commandments are too restricting and they cost more than one can pay, I hope to show you how misguided that notion is. It's not trying to satisfy God's law at the center of this excuse, it's not being able to do all the sinful things people find pleasure in doing without breaking them that is causing the complaints.

We are so wrapped up in our own lives and in the things that we find bring us pleasure. It doesn't matter if this pleasure is so short-lived, and we must renew our efforts to find it on a daily basis. We are willing to do so, so why should God tell us not to? We need to understand the law was given not to deprive us of these things, it is to protect us from the things we do that cause us harm. The law also provides people protection from each other in case we disobey. God gave us guidelines to protect us; not to deprive us.

On the flip side of this equation, we give the excuse that we don't want to start doing things we are not doing already. This can be anything from attending church services, reading a Bible, praying, or fellowshipping with other believers. These activities come to mind when we think of accepting Christianity as our life. It seems like there will be such an upheaval in our life it would not be worth the undertaking. The truth is so much better than this misunderstanding, but it is hard for a non-believer to see the truth.

It is true our lives will change dramatically—completely even. But what is not true is believing it will not be worth it. For you who are searching, I wish I could make you understand how much more your lives will be worth once you have accepted Christ! It is a difficult thing to do, when you haven't experienced the growth of salvation. But, we who are saved must make every effort to show those who aren't how wonderful this new life really is; and we must do so with our walk.

We who are believers need to display how much satisfaction we receive from the fulfilling of our calling to participate in these activities that appear to be burdens to the non-believer. This is the best way I know of to remove this preconception that there are burdens to begin with. If we do this, the chance that others will overcome this stumbling block is much improved. So let us strive to do so to the best of our abilities, and follow the Holy Spirit's leading in this area of living a life others will also desire to live.

In talking about the Ten Commandments and the importance of our obedience to them, I know how difficult it is to accept them as God's protective law when one is not a believer. I remember well how it was for myself. The Word makes no sense to the non-believer and this is something many believers do not take into account. Non-believers will not be able to make sense of it. They will not understand it. It is foolishness to them, and they believe we who follow God's Word are fools. But for those who profess to be a believer, the trusting and believing in the Bible should not be foolishness to you.

I am not saying it should be easy to live your life by these Ten Commandments. On your own it is impossible, but if you are truly saved, and have accepted Christ, then you have received the Holy Spirit in your heart and you won't have to do it on your own. With His help, we will know when we break His commandments, and we will be able to repent for doing so. Even though we will still fall, we ask God to forgive us when we do. That's the difference Christ makes in our lives.

If you feel you are a true believer, and yet you still feel you cannot live the Christian life, I want you to re-examine yourself. Is it possible you are truly saved and have received the Holy Spirit in your heart, but have not taken the next step of surrendering control of your life over to Him? Jesus enters our hearts when we repent and believe in His sacrifice on the Cross, but He does not forcefully take over our lives. We have to allow Him to do so and we have to ask Him to do so.

If you find yourself in the category of believing but not living accordingly, then this could well be one of the problems holding you back. Ask the Holy Spirit to lead, and then follow. If He tells you something must be removed from your life, then remove it. If He says something must be added, go and get it. We must pay attention to His words, and then follow His instructions.

If we are truly honest with ourselves, it's not hard to see this excuse is really nothing more than a refusal to give up the importance of our own "self." We want to believe we are the most important thing in our life, and therefore, whatever we want to do or not do is okay by us. This egotistical stumbling block creates the superficial reason for this excuse. The question is whether or not we can admit that our excuse is selfishness. If we can, it's a lot easier to overcome the root of the problem. It can be as simple as admitting this truth to ourselves, and to our God. If we do this, we can reach a point where instead of wanting to do things we shouldn't, we will want to do the things we should.

Price Tag #3: Shame or Embarrassment

So many of those who are thinking about a life with Christ are too caught up in yet another excuse that they don't want to suffer the embarrassment. This comes from a perception the world has generated over the centuries; Christians are simple-minded people who are easily fooled. We are shown through the media how Christians are lacking in areas on which the secularists place much value. The non-believer doesn't want to pay that price tag of possible embarrassment because he's afraid of being inferior in traits like intelligence and ambition, and doesn't want to be looked down upon because of others' perceptions.

A more accurate way to describe this condition is to say people who feel this way are ashamed of God, the Gospel, and Jesus Christ. God's Word is very explicit about this condition, as we see in Mark 8:38; "If anyone is ashamed of me and my words in this adulterous and sinful generation, the Son of Man will be ashamed of him when he comes in his Father's glory with the holy angels." This was a warning issued by Jesus Christ for us, because He knew this would be a consequence of the world's efforts to discredit Him and His Church.

This form of dismissing Christianity from our lives is a very personal one. It's very hard for someone to share this feeling of shame we can have when others ask if we are a believer. But if we are honest with ourselves, we know we have all felt something like it at some time in our walk, and that honesty can help others understand and believe too. We do not want others to know we are embarrassed to call ourselves Christians, especially if we are professing ourselves to be true believers. I believe this is one of the more subtle methods satan employs against us; it is very simple but all too often it is effective.

I remember as a young man how I felt this embarrassment in my own life. I was being called by God to make a commitment to His Son, but I was consumed by the shame I would experience because of how my close companions would feel towards me if I went ahead with it. Many times I felt the pull on my heart after a sermon invited me to receive God's gift of salvation; but there was no way I would let my friends see me fall for it. Yes, I know what it means to be ashamed of our Lord.

By no means is this only a trouble spot for youth; it is something many never grow out of. As adults, we find ourselves reasoning our way through this difficulty as well. It takes on new forms, but the root problem is still the same: we are ashamed of the gospel of Christ. God's Word warns us once again in Romans 1:16; "I am not ashamed of the gospel, because it is the power of God for the salvation of everyone who believes: first for the Jew, then for the Gentile." This passage has been given to warn us of a condition that will attack us. When we sit down and read God's Word for our personal growth, we find these types of warnings and answers for everything we shall ever encounter in our life. There is no limit to the value we get from reading our Bibles prayerfully; they are priceless!

It's time to be honest with each other. I will share some of the ways in which this problem showed itself in my own walk, and you may have experienced the same ones. But, there are many possibilities out there, so take the time to discover which ones may have attacked you in the past or may be doing so in the present. This is a way believers can help each other overcome our difficulties, and we must support each other to make our walks easier. The key is we must learn to recognize them for what they are: ways we can feel ashamed of our faith in Christ and the Christian life He offers.

One of the most obvious examples of this shame showed itself in the way I would shy away from mentioning any specific area of my Christian life with others. When an opportunity would present itself, and I would feel the Holy Spirit attempting to prod me forward in a witnessing mode, I would allow a spirit of fear to creep into my heart. This fearful attitude would prevent me from presenting the Gospel. I tried for years to dismiss this problem as being a result of my personality. I thought I was too shy for verbal witnessing. How easily we reason things out for ourselves when we want to. Do you know what I mean?

It would be better for us to step back, and take a closer look at what is really happening when we fall victim to those feelings of shame leading to a fearful attitude. This spirit of fear comes to us from satan, and it is only with the guidance of the Holy Spirit we will ever overcome it. On our own we are too weak to do it, so we must learn to lean on our Counselor. That is why He is here—to champion our cause. We must realize the fact that when we are afraid to share our faith, the most likely reason is because of this sense of shame towards letting others know that we are Christians.

I understand there are going to be some people with introverted personalities not allowing them to share their faith with others as well as they may desire. I am not speaking to these types of believers, I am talking to the ones of us who reflect in our minds, and come to the understanding there is this inkling of embarrassment stopping us. We need to be aware of the fact it is more than just an embarrassment; it is a shameful feeling. This is the feeling we are warned about once more by the Scriptures in 2 Timothy 1:8; "So do not be ashamed to testify about our Lord, or ashamed of me his prisoner. But join with me in suffering for the gospel, by the power of God." We must follow those instructions in order to help others.

A method of overcoming which worked for me was to mention specific areas of my church life such as a musical presentation that was going to be performed at church. Maybe there is a Christmas nativity play that your church puts on, or a church picnic. These are topics we can bring up more casually, and they can open the door for further discussions with your friends and co-workers. It's not as hard to talk about deeper subjects if we are asked about them after setting the stage through bringing up easier things to talk about first. It is definitely harder to initiate these topics without first setting the stage, that's for sure.

Setting the stage for discussions on salvation is so important for us to do. There is nothing more important in somebody's life than whether or not they receive forgiveness for their sins and spend eternity with God in heaven. God's Word says in Romans 10:14–15:

> How, then, can they call on the one they have not believed in? And how can they believe in the one of whom they have not heard? And how can they hear without someone preaching to them? And how can they preach unless they are sent? As it is written, 'How beautiful are the feet of those who bring good news!'

Those beautiful feet should belong to all believers; we are the ones meant to share the good news about our Lord with all of those around us.

Another example present in my own life was the embarrassment I would feel if I tried to pray out loud in church, Sunday school, or even simply giving thanks for a meal at home when others were present, let alone in public at a restaurant. Perhaps this is something you are experiencing in your own life. I believe it is very common because many people have mentioned this in their own experiences.

As I said earlier, some of you may be so introverted in your personality you simply cannot pray in public; however, you are not the ones I am talking about. I am talking about people more like myself. I did not have any trouble talking in public. It was simply the act of praying causing me this embarrassment factor. The trick in overcoming this condition for me was recognizing what was really going on in my mind when I felt that nervous sensation leading to my embarrassment.

When I stepped back and looked deep into my own heart, I came to the realization my fear of sharing was just another way I felt embarrassed of my Christianity. I know this statement is a strong one, but at least in my own walk, it was true. I tried to figure out why I could speak about secular topics in public settings without getting tongue-tied, and yet I could not do the same with spiritual ones. Prayer was just another example of the horribly embarrassing shame I believed I would suffer for letting others know about my personal relationship with God. Once I recognized what was causing my problem, I asked for God's help, and it was a lot easier to overcome.

These problematic embarrassment issues can be beneficial when they cause you to recognize the root of a troublesome area in your own walk, because the recognition will lead to a solution to the problem and victory over embarrassment. Whenever I feel myself heading towards that old sensation of being shamefully embarrassed, I immediately step back and look to discover what is causing me to feel like this. It is always satan, as he tries to deceive us so we are not able to bear fruit in our Christian life. Whatever we are embarrassed about, we can have victory over it when we let the Holy Spirit shine through us and we are obedient to His leading.

In your own life, you may experience other areas tending to cause this shameful embarrassment. It does not matter what they are. What matters is your understanding of them; they are times in your walk when you are being tempted to be ashamed of Christ. I challenge you to consider carefully whether or not this is true in your own case. Maybe it's not so; maybe you are one of the introverts whose inner makeup simply won't allow speaking in public for any reason. I am writing this for those who can speak publicly, as long as it's not about Jesus Christ and the Good News of salvation. That was the state I found myself in, and if you have a similar experience, I urge you to do as I did—step back and look deeply into your heart. Is there more going on there than just simply a fear of public speaking?

Ask yourself that question. Ask the Holy Spirit the same question and He will answer you. If you receive an answer convicting you, then heed the warnings I shared from God's Word. Do not be ashamed of our Lord, and overcome satan's efforts to hinder your walk. Do not ignore the warnings given in Scripture, because if you do you run the risk of having our Lord be ashamed of you when you stand before Him in Heaven; that is not a risk we should be willing to take.

Price Tag #4: Lifestyle Change

One other excuse involving a price tag to pay when considering your salvation is the giving up of friends and activities. This is another excuse I have often heard when asking others the reasons behind their choice not to accept God's gift of salvation. The thing we must keep in mind when we are bothered by this is that whatever changes we are led to make will be for our own benefit.

When we are led to Christ, all things about our lives are changed. Though we are not literally born-again in the physical sense, we are completely born-again in the spiritual sense. God's Word says in 2 Corinthians 5:17; "Therefore, if anyone is in Christ, he is a new creation; the old has gone, the new has come!" This fact is the key; we must remember our old friends will not be changed, it is us who have been changed when we accept God's gift.

This doesn't mean we will not be able to maintain

friendships we had prior to conversion. We will make each determination on an individual basis, not as a generalization. We will find there will be some people we associated with, and some activities we participated in, that as new creations, we simply don't want to be involved with any longer. You will find this is the case when you realize certain people were only involved with you when you were participating in what you now know is a sinful activity. If you are honest with yourself, you will admit you knew some of these activities were sinful before your conversion. As a new creation, you just can't choose to ignore this understanding any longer. You will pass on the old things you know will only cause you to stumble in your new walk. The wonderful thing is, many of your old friends may want to follow you when they see the joy in your heart coming from your new life in Christ. You may end up growing closer to some of them than you ever were before! Praise God!

Admittedly, it is a sad thought to think of leaving some old friends and old activities behind. However, I want you to be assured your life will not be empty because of it. You will be gaining new friends, fellow believers, and together you will find joy in new activities. You might be doing some of the same things you were before, but the way you participate in them may be different. This may be something as simple as enjoying an event without becoming intoxicated while doing so, and I'm sure you can think of other examples. This is just one example of the changes coming in your new life. Just remember: they will all be for your personal benefit and spiritual growth.

This is one of the most magnificent changes I have experienced: friends can be close, but when they are believers we fellowship with, they are closer still. The fellow believers you will meet will be more than just friends; they will be mentors and disciples for you. They will help you move forward in your newfound faith, and you will help them as well. You are going to find fellowship with these friends is more enjoyable than any activity you participated in before you were saved.

If any activity you were involved in before salvation is now understood to be of a sinful nature, you will eventually stop being involved with it. However, in your newly created state, to walk away from such activities will hurt a lot less than you would expect. We put away the sinful things from our past, and replace them with things acceptable to our God. This does not mean we cannot enjoy the things we do. Quite the contrary, you will enjoy the new activities much more than you did the old ones.

You will find yourself happier in your new activities, and completely at ease in your fellowshipping with other believers. Your life will be much more fulfilling, and you will find the inner peace we are promised in Philippians 4:4–9:

> Rejoice in the Lord always. I will say it again: Rejoice! Let your gentleness be evident to all. The Lord is near. Do not be anxious about anything, but in everything, by prayer and petition, with thanksgiving, present your requests to God. And the peace of God, which transcends all understanding, will guard your hearts and your minds in Christ Jesus.
>
> Finally, brothers, whatever is true, whatever is noble, whatever is right, whatever is pure, whatever is lovely, whatever is admirable—if anything is excellent or praiseworthy—think about such things. Whatever you

> have learned or received or heard from me—put into practice. And the God of peace will be with you.

I want you to know this passage, like every other passage in God's Word, is true! I can personally tell you this one is true because I have felt this peace God promised to us. I testify to you, anything or anyone you may feel compelled to give up from your prior life will pale in comparison to whatever or whomever comes into your new life as a replacement.

Your whole life will be a witness to them as they see the profound changes taking place in your life before their very eyes. Once you become secure in your new walk, you will begin to witness to the friends you had before. It will be one of the most fulfilling times when you lead one of your old friends to Christ. I have never, and I promise you will never, look back with regret for having left the old life for your new one with Christ.

Chapter Four

I'm Not Worthy of Salvation

Unworthiness as an excuse for not accepting Christianity is the one which saddens me the most when I hear it. When you abide by the unworthy excuse, it's like saying to God, "The sacrifice of your beloved Son wasn't enough for me. What else have you got?"

People who use the unworthiness excuse believe their act and walk is so heinous, there is no way God would possibly ever forgive them. They actually go a step farther and believe there is no way God could possibly forgive them. How sad this condition is, and how mistaken this belief. It breaks my heart knowing someone who feels this way is right; they don't deserve to be saved by God. But what they haven't realized is the fact that none of us deserve it! They are no worse than the rest of us, and we will be looking at proof of this fact in this chapter.

I hesitate to call it an excuse, because it is more of a

misunderstanding of human nature, but it has been mentioned by people I have questioned, so here it is. I try to make them understand this particular excuse is nothing more than a horrible misunderstanding of God's Word, and if they will take the time to examine the Scriptures, they will discover they are wrong to believe as they do.

There are several different conditions falling into this category of unworthiness, but before looking at them, we need to learn the definition of the word itself. According to Webster's, *unworthiness* means to be lacking of any value or excellence. It is a baseless condition marked by dishonor, and being proven poor and worthless. It also means to be without merit, and undeserving of attention.

The condition of unworthiness is real. In our fallen state we are all truly unworthy of the grace, love, forgiveness, mercy and sacrifice of so great a God; but that is what's so great about God. When we were still lost in our sin He died for us. God's Word tells us this fact in Romans 5:8; "But God demonstrates His own love for us in this: While we were yet sinners, Christ died for us."

If we examine ourselves and admit to the truths we find, we will realize all of us are unworthy. Who could be worthy in reality in the presence of a Holy God? Unworthiness does not just include the worst of us...no one is worthy of God's love and forgiveness. That is the reason I feel so saddened by those believing unworthiness is a reason to not search for God's grace. They are missing one of the greatest truths God has given us in the Scriptures, and it is the calling of all believers to help them understand that we all have fallen short and are unworthy.

God's Word says in the book of Romans 3:23; "for all have sinned and fall short of the glory of God." How much more specific could our Lord have been in telling us which ones of us fall into categories such as unworthiness and unrighteousness? Each and every one of us who has ever been born, is currently alive, or ever will be; God meant all of us when He said, "all of us have sinned and fallen short" of His glory. He didn't say some of us failed, or most of us failed. He said all of us have failed!

Our failure started in the beginning, as God's Word says in the book of Genesis 3:1–7:

> Now the serpent was more crafty than any of the wild animals the Lord God had made. He said to the woman, "Did God really say, 'You must not eat from any tree in the garden'?"
>
> The woman said to the serpent, "We may eat fruit from the trees in the garden, but God did say, 'You must not eat fruit from the tree that is in the middle of the garden, and you must not touch it, or you will die.'"
>
> "You will not surely die," the serpent said to the woman. "For God knows that when you eat of it your eyes will be opened, and you will be like God, knowing good and evil."
>
> When the woman saw that the fruit of the tree was good for food and pleasing to the eye, and also desirable for gaining wisdom, she took some and ate it. She also gave some to her husband, who was with her, and he ate it. Then the eyes of both of them were opened, and they realized they were naked; so they sewed fig leaves together and made coverings for themselves.

From then on, we have all been unworthy; however, God in His amazing love for us reached out to mankind and offered us the hope of receiving forgiveness in the same way Adam had lost it—through one man. Scripture tells us this in Romans 5:18–19:

> Consequently, just as the result of one trespass was condemnation for all men, so also the result of one act of righteousness was justification that brings life for all men. For just as through the disobedience of the one man (Adam) the many were made sinners, so also through the obedience of the one man (Jesus Christ) the many will be made righteous.

I hope we are beginning to see how none of us are less worthwhile than any others. But if not, God's Word is full of passages to help us. There are more than I could ever list, so by no means could I ever exhaust all of them here in this book. We find another similar passage in Romans 3:10–12; "As it is written: There is no one righteous, not even one; there is no one who understands, no one who seeks God. All have turned away, they have together become worthless; there is no one who does good, not even one."

The Apostle Paul has made it perfectly clear for us here: there has not been a single person on Earth who was worthy of being called righteous before God. Our Lord Jesus is the only one who has ever been qualified for this title—no one else. It is said that misery loves company, and in this area of unworthiness we have the whole of mankind for company. So we should never feel we are somehow of lesser value than another, because Scripture says the exact opposite is true.

Another passage to read is found in the book of 1 Timothy 1:15–16:

> Here is a trustworthy saying that deserves full acceptance: Christ Jesus came into the world to save sinners—of whom I am the worst. But for that very reason I was shown mercy so that in me, the worst of sinners, Christ Jesus might display his unlimited patience as an example for those who would believe on him and receive eternal life.

What a powerful statement! This was written for us by Paul, a man who had persecuted the Christian church to the point of killing those who were believers. He is pointing out for us that no matter how unworthy we may feel, he considers himself to be the least worthy of all due to his persecution of Christ's followers after the Crucifixion.

Before his conversion, Paul was a member of a religious group believing Christ and His followers were all evil people. They believed Christians should be stopped at all costs, including death. So, he traveled in pursuit of believers to throw them into prison for trial and execution. While on one of these trips, the Lord Jesus Christ told him to stop persecuting His people. From that day on, Paul began serving the very people he had been persecuting. It was because of his destructive behavior Paul considered himself to be the worst of all sinners. He is throwing down a challenge to any who may consider themselves unworthy of Christ's forgiveness: who among you can claim to be a worse sinner than I was?

Another passage where we find God loving us even though we don't deserve it is Romans 5:6–8:

> You see, at just the right time, when we were still powerless, Christ died for the ungodly. Very rarely will anyone die for a righteous man, though for a good

> man someone might possibly dare to die. But God demonstrates His own love for us in this: While we were yet sinners, Christ died for us.

What an amazing statement this is. Christ died for us even though we did not deserve it! It was done for us out of the love God has for us; no other reason can explain it. We did not earn this gift of salvation, it was freely given. There was nothing we could do to receive it back then, and there is nothing we can do now either! God sent His Son into the world to die on the Cross so we could be saved by grace.

Another example of why it is futile to attempt to prove ourselves worthy is found in Romans 7:18–20:

> I know that nothing good lives in me, that is, in my sinful nature. For I have the desire to do what is good, but I cannot carry it out. For what I do is not the good I want to do; no, the evil I do not want to do—this I keep on doing. Now if I do what I do not want to do, it is no longer I who do it, but it is sin living in me that does it.

An accurate description for this sin inside of us is found in James 4:17; "Anyone, then, who knows the good he ought to do and doesn't do it, sins." These two passages make it clear that none of us are worthy of being called righteous. Without God, we fail miserably in living a life trying to qualify us as being righteous. When we are honest with ourselves, we know exactly what Paul meant about not doing the good things we intend to do. How often do we find ourselves doing the bad things we don't intend to do? This is not a condition existing in some of us; we have now seen it is true for all of us!

The theme which runs throughout these passages of Scripture is *none* of us. None of us are righteous, none of us are good, none of us are deserving, and we are all guilty of sin; yet, Christ died for us! There is no one who is so unworthy they cannot receive this gift of salvation offered through Christ's death on the Cross. This is the thing we must understand: there is no one who is so horrible, so undeserving, so wicked, or so beyond redemption they cannot be saved! We were all unworthy, but we are all offered the same gift of salvation. The only difference remaining between each of us is whether we have received this gift or not.

Before moving into specific areas of unworthiness, I want to remind you that when looking at this excuse, we must remember these words from Romans 3:10–12; "As it is written: 'There is no one righteous, not even one; there is no one who understands, no one who seeks God. All have turned away, they have together become worthless; there is no one who does good, not even one.'" If we burn those words into our hearts, we can overcome our feeling unworthy of God's love and His gift of salvation. God will forgive us no matter what our offences and shortcomings may be. Never forget that!

Common Unworthiness Reasoning:
I'm Unworthy in Others' Eyes

One particular feeling of unworthiness which is very difficult to overcome is the type put into place through others saying you are worthless and you will never amount to anything. It is so sad how we can be put into such a pitiful disposition by the comments of people around us, but it happens all the time. Comments mentioned, no matter how innocently they were said, can have a sharpness that pounds the person on the receiving end of them.

The worst of all the cases I have found have been when a parent or a loved one is the person delivering the damaging comments. Looking back, I remember doing this to my own family at different times during my children's growing-up periods. I give thanks to God for helping me to stop treating my children that way. As parents, we can never give our children enough positive reinforcements, but with God's help, we will always do better.

Unfortunately, this is not the case in a lot of families. There have been too many times when I was in a position to overhear a parent berating a child. We've all witnessed this in the grocery store, at children's sporting events, walking through a subdivision, or at school activities. It is one of the saddest facts of family life in our country today, and the worst thing of all, there is no end in sight to this type of behavior.

Comments I once used and still hear are, "You don't know anything; you're nothing but a brat; you'll never amount to anything; you are so stupid." We don't mean to hurt our children by saying them, but sometimes we do anyway. This is a great example of what the Apostle Paul meant in Romans 7:18–20, which we looked at earlier in this chapter.

It's easy to see how much more damaging negative comments are when coming from parents and those we love. I don't mean to diminish the amount of damage done by others in our lives, only to stress the extreme damage done when it is by the ones we are closest to. When around our loved ones, we put our guards down and are most vulnerable. We are the most open to the influence, whether good or bad, of our family members and other loved ones.

I can't stress enough how important it is for those of us

responsible for raising our children not to burden them with a sense of having no self worth. God's Word tells us in Colossians 3:21; "Fathers, do not embitter your children, or they may become discouraged." It's very hard for them to overcome the emotional damage, and some never do. So, don't tell your loved ones they will never amount to anything, or they are not good for anything, or make any comments similar to these. The damage could stay with them for the rest of their lives, so avoid doing this at all costs.

As for the ones who are suffering with these feelings of unworthiness, I know it is very difficult to do, but you must listen to what the Scriptures tell us. The Word of God says there is no one who is worthy. It does not say some are worthy and some aren't. It does not say some are less worthy than others, and it does not say there are special people who are more worthy than others. Just remember what it does say; none are righteous, not even one, and this is true for those who belittle you, too.

I've Sinned Too Much

There is another group of people out there believing they have done something in their life so bad, so absolutely horrendous, beyond telling, it's therefore beyond forgiveness. This is another difficult problem to overcome because it is hard to get someone to even mention they suffer with it. The shame they feel in themselves is so strong, they will not open up and share their pain and suffering. They suffer from the false notion of having committed what they believe to be an unforgivable sin. You can see why that makes this condition difficult to deal with, because they've been left to deal with it on their own because of this shame they suffer.

When looking at this problem area, when you actually share a shameful dark spot, you don't have to confess it to other men to be forgiven. As believers, we are told to confess our sins to God, repent from committing them, and He will forgive us. This is found in I John 1:9; "If we confess our sins, he is faithful and just and will forgive us our sins and purify us from all unrighteousness."

Confessing our sin is just an admission to God of the evil intent existing in our hearts. Repentance is the "changing direction" of our heart toward God and His righteousness. We can say with our mouths we have repented, but our actions and attitudes will only reflect our sincerity when we have truly repented in our hearts.

You don't have to share specific details of your sin with others unless you feel it may help you. If there is someone trying to help you in this area, they should be able to do so by using concepts instead of specifics. I believe it is a dangerous thing to ask for details of another person's sin, because we run the risk of falling in the same way as they did when we do. God's Word warns against this in Galatians 6:1; "Brothers, if someone is caught in a sin, you who are spiritual should restore him gently. But watch yourself, or you also may be tempted." Based on this passage, I don't believe it's necessary to go beyond generalities in sharing with each other.

Using this concept of generalities, we won't bother to list any group of sinful behaviors here. The process of repentance is the same for all sin, regardless of how different our individual sins may be in our own eyes. But, no matter how different particular sins appear to us, they all appear the same to God.

God's Word teaches this in the book of James 2:8–11:

> If you really keep the royal law found in scripture, "Love your neighbor as yourself," you are doing right. But if you show favoritism, you sin and are convicted by the law as lawbreakers. For whoever keeps the whole law and yet stumbles at just one point is guilty of breaking all of it. For He who said, "Do not commit adultery," also said "Do not murder." If you do not commit adultery but do commit murder you have become a lawbreaker.

To understand this passage fully, we need to remember what Christ said when teaching about murder and adultery, which we read earlier in Matthew 5:21–22 and 27–30. He told us if we become angry with our brother we are guilty of murder in our heart. He also said if we look at someone and lust after them in our heart, we are guilty of adultery. It's very important we understand you don't have to commit the physical act to be guilty; the desire in our hearts condemns us, and no physical actions are required.

With that in mind, let's go back to our passage from James 2:8–11. James is telling us no matter how satisfactorily we are able to follow some of the law, or most of the law, or almost all of the law, if we still manage to trip up and fall under one part of the law, we are guilty in all of it. He did not tell us if it's only some small matter we are guilty of, we are somehow less guilty than those who fall in some major matter. Scripture doesn't tell us there is a rating scale for our sins. It tells us all of them lead to death. Knowing all sins lead to death, why would people believe one particular sin makes them unforgivable? I believe it is because they don't understand God's Word in this area, and I hope I am able to help them see the truth.

Two more places we can turn in God's Word are 1 John 3:4;

"Everyone who sins breaks the law; in fact, sin is lawlessness." Then in 1 John 1:8 we are told; "If we claim to be without sin, we deceive ourselves and the truth is not in us." Putting these two verses together, we are told if any of us claim not to sin, we are liars. We are also told everyone who sins is guilty of breaking the law. So the teaching we should get from these verses is that all of us are lawbreakers, and we are all guilty of sin. Since we have already learned all sins deserve punishment, now we know you do not have to commit what we call a heinous type to be found guilty.

The Apostle Paul called himself the worst of sinners because of his zealous persecution of the Christians right after the Crucifixion of Christ. There have been countless others who probably felt qualified to use that title; however, Scripture tells us no matter what the offense might be, the blood of Jesus can wash it away. This is found in Isaiah 1:18; "'Come now, let us reason together,' says the Lord. 'Though your sins are like scarlet, they shall be as white as snow; though they are red as crimson, they shall be like wool.'"

To put this in perspective for modern times, it means individuals who were guilty of the most horrific crimes of modern history such as Adolph Hitler or Joseph Stalin, would have been saved by the blood of Christ if they truly confessed, repented, and asked God to forgive them of their sins. We are not condemned because of the frequency with which we commit a sin; it is because of our failure to confess our sins to God and repent of them that we stand condemned.

When I try to explain that there is no one who cannot be saved by grace, I like to use the Roman soldiers who actually nailed Jesus on the Cross as a perfect example. I have a hard time imagining any crime greater than being the one to drive those nails into His hands and feet, or to have been one of the Jews shouting for Him to be crucified. Imagine standing there watching Him die, feeling a sense of accomplishment for ridding the earth of Him. What greater crime could one commit? And yet even these people all had the opportunity to accept His gift of salvation if they confessed, repented, and asked for forgiveness. Whatever dark stain you may have on your heart can't possibly eclipse what those people were guilty of. So lift your head up, and look to your Father in Heaven. He is ready to save you if you just ask Him.

I'm Too Insignificant

The next example of unworthiness people have shared with me, deals with the feeling of simply being too insignificant to be worth God's attention. This is another condition that may have been caused by other people making them feel this way, or it may be a self-inflicted one.

To learn what God says about this condition, let's turn to the book of Genesis 1:26–28. "Then God said, 'Let us make man in our image, in our likeness and let them rule over the fish of the sea and the birds of the air, over the livestock, over all the earth, and over all the creatures that move along the ground.'" Here, God shows how valuable man was from the beginning of Creation. We were given control over all of the Earth, and everything placed on it. God valued us over everything else He created. Another place where God talks about the value of man is found in the book of Luke 12:24; "Consider the ravens: They do now sow or reap, they have no storeroom or barn; yet God feeds them. And how much more valuable you are than birds!" Here, we are reminded how the birds of the air do not have to sow or reap in order to be fed by God. We are told how much more valuable we are than the birds of the air, so we should not worry about such things because God will surely supply us with all we need.

Another similar passage is found in Matthew 10:29–31; "Are not two sparrows sold for a penny? Yet not one of them will fall to the ground apart from the will of your Father. And even the very hairs of your head are all numbered. So don't be afraid; you are worth more than many sparrows." Jesus says we are worth much more than the sparrows; and even the hairs on our heads are numbered by God. This shows us how important we are to God. Imagine knowing the number of hairs on one person's head let alone on every human that has ever been born!

If you are having trouble believing you are worth God's attention, then just think about how these Scriptures say the opposite is true. God has shown He values our souls so much He sent His only Son to die on the Cross in order for us to be able to have a relationship with Him. Jesus Christ suffered and died for us because His Father asked Him to, and God asked Him to because He does value man over the rest of His creation.

You are worth more to God than you can imagine. Two places to find these truths are in the book of John 3:16; "For God so loved the world that he gave his one and only Son, that whoever believes in him shall not perish but have eternal life." Also in Luke 22:42; "Father, if you are willing, take this cup from me; yet not my will, but yours be done."

To believe we are not worth God's attention is going directly against the Word of God. We are all worth more to God than anything else under the sun. I can sympathize with anyone who feels like these passages are just too simple to be true, but that is the beauty of Scripture. If we just look at them, we find the Bible is meant to be easily understood. We suffer from a tendency to complicate things, making it harder for us to gain the insight God placed so plainly in His Word.

I'm Physically Unworthy

The next category comes from the person who feels they are unworthy because of some physical trait. There are so many different natures of this type to be found, ranging from being overweight, feeling unattractive, having a handicap, and so on. All of them have one characteristic in common: the people who feel this way are convinced that whatever their perceived defect might be, it makes them unworthy of being loved by anyone else. They end up including God in this equation, while His Word says this isn't possible.

We must be careful not to let ourselves become like the religious leaders who were scolded in Matthew 23:27; "Woe to you teachers of the law and Pharisees, you hypocrites! You are like whitewashed tombs, which look beautiful on the outside, but on the inside are full of dead men's bones and everything unclean." Pharisees were religious rulers who kept themselves clean as a way of proving their righteousness. Jesus saw how perfect they were on the outside, but how ugly they were on the inside.

Jesus scolded them again in Luke 16:15; "He said to them, 'You are the ones who justify yourselves in the eyes of men, but God knows your hearts. What is highly valued among men is detestable in God's sight.'"

We have all heard the saying "beauty is only skin-deep," but these two passages prove this saying is not true. People's true beauty is found below the surface of the skin; it is found in their hearts. If we walk around and look at the outer layer of people to see their beauty, we are not looking in the way

God does. We need to remember that since God doesn't place significance on someone's outer beauty, neither should we.

This same fact must be used to cover another type of physically identifiable trait separating people; the color of our skin. Here, I alter the saying just a little bit, and it becomes "color is only skin deep." This is an area I personally find disgusting—placing the value of someone to the color of his or her skin. I ask, by whose standards are they making this judgment of someone's worth? It certainly has nothing to do with God's Word, for it goes against everything taught in the Scriptures.

To tackle this terrible condition of prejudice, and to show how horribly wrong it is, I will start with the people on the receiving end of this treatment. I realize I can never truly know the pain and anguish this prejudice has caused and is causing people of color, and I don't mean to imply that I do. But, I do want to extend my deepest sympathies to all who have been touched by this evil spirit. That is what I consider it to be: evil showing itself through one ethnic group of people attacking another.

This type of prejudice is not limited to skin color as it may include nationality, religious sect, level of education, income level, political affiliation, and a host of other differences found between different groups or classes of people. No matter what the particular difference is between the two groups involved, it always ends in a mistaken idea that one of the groups is superior to the other. Furthermore, the other group must be made to consider themselves inferior in order to perpetuate the lie.

For those of you who have found yourselves on this receiving end, I applaud all who have managed to rise above this falsehood thrown upon you. You are to be commended, for you are contributing to the banishment of this prejudicial belief system which has existed for way too long. As for those who have fallen victim by believing there is any truth in whatever criteria is being used to establish a superior/inferior condition, God's Word is going to show you how you have been duped into accepting a lie.

As we should in all matters, we will turn again to the Scriptures to see what God has said on this matter of prejudice. If we study our Bibles, we will find that according to the Scriptures there are only two types of people in the world. One is the Jew. They are the chosen people from whom God separated for Himself among all the peoples in the world. This started when God called out a man named Abram, as found in the book of Genesis 12:1–2:

> The Lord had said to Abram, "Leave your country, your people and your father's household and go to the land I will show you. I will make you into a great nation and I will bless you; I will make your name great, and you will be a blessing."

Later, God blessed Abram with a son, and changed his name to Abraham, which means "father of many nations."

From Abraham on, all of his descendants have been called the Jewish people. They are the ones God called out from the rest, and that is why they are called the "chosen people." All the other people in the world are known as the "gentiles," which simply means they are not direct descendants of Abraham. These are the only two possibilities we can find ourselves belonging to according to Scripture. This area of history also lends itself as a tool of prejudice, but a peculiar one at that. Both sides of the equation have used their heritage against the other, and at times it is hard to tell which one is the abuser and which is the victim.

God's Word tells us what difference He sees between the Jews and the Gentiles, and this answer is found in the book of Romans 10:12–13; "For there is no difference between Jew and Gentile—the same Lord is Lord of all and richly blesses all who call on Him, for 'Everyone who calls on the name of the Lord will be saved.' "

God's Word is perfectly clear as we read that passage from Romans, there is no inherent difference between the only two groups of people listed in the Bible. Both of these groups have the same Lord, and both of them are offered the same gift of salvation. Both of them will receive the same gift if they fulfill the requirements to receive it, and both of them will suffer the same condemnation if they refuse it. Praise God for making His Word simple enough for us to understand!

So, if someone says your race or ethnic group is somehow inferior to another, just memorize this Scripture and burn it on your heart. Do not let yourself be tricked into believing such lies in even the slightest form, because they are nothing more than lies no matter what form they may take. Rise above them, and you too will become one of the positive factors for ridding the world of them. It is very difficult for these prejudices to continue if the subjects of the falsehoods cannot be convinced they have one iota of truth in them. This does not mean you have a right to turn the prejudice around, that's not what I am implying. If you do, you will be just as guilty of prejudice as they are, which is why we say, "Two wrongs will not make a right"—it's true.

Now turning to those on the delivering end of whatever prejudice you may be involved in, we will look at what God has to say to you. Turn to the book of Proverbs 8:13; "To fear the

Lord is to hate evil; I hate pride and arrogance, evil behavior and perverse speech." This verse is very appropriate to study when questioning prejudicial behavior. The person who is guilty of this offense is also guilty of the sin of pride. We are going to focus our attention and look at the root cause of all prejudice: the presence of pride in an individual.

This pride may be something in relation to race, color, body size and shape, level of attractiveness, nationality, particular denomination of religion, educational level, political affiliation, or any other unique personal trait we find in ourselves. In order to overcome the spirit of prejudice, we must first recognize the false sense of pride creating the arrogant behavior in us.

Much of this pride has developed in us from our upbringing. Your parents may have tried to give you a healthy sense of pride in yourself and your heritage. I believe this is a natural tendency in parents to want their children to be proud of themselves, but we must be very careful to never use comments such as, "You are much smarter than...,You are much prettier than...,"or anything else along those same lines. This is the way prejudice repeats itself from generation to generation. Remember, it is the general principle I am stressing and not a particular offense. There is no difference in God's eyes between any of them; they are all evil.

One can sympathize, to some extent, with those who are not in the brotherhood of believers and are guilty of this offense. They have no standard to look up to other than the one this world has taught them. We cannot expect to hold them up to the standards our God has established in His Word, because to the unbeliever, His standards are but foolishness. However, there is no excuse to be found for anyone who claims to be a believer and yet is still guilty of this ugly condition. We make some allowance for a newly born believer, but they should change their behavior immediately once they are taught God's Word. This should serve as one of the proofs of their salvation: leaving behind these types of prideful ways and the sinful behaviors to which they lead.

The best example I can think of to illustrate this point comes from Philippians 3: 4–9:

> Though I myself have reasons for such confidence. If anyone else thinks he has reasons to put confidence in the flesh, I have more: circumcised on the eighth day, of the people of Israel, of the tribe of Benjamin, a Hebrew of Hebrews; in regard to the law, a Pharisee; as for zeal, persecuting the church; as for legalistic righteousness, faultless. But whatever was to my profit I now consider loss for the sake of Christ. What is more, I consider everything a loss compared to the surpassing greatness of knowing Christ Jesus my Lord, for whose sake I have lost all things. I consider them rubbish, that I may gain Christ and be found in him, not having a righteousness of my own that comes from the law, but that which is through faith in Christ—the righteousness that comes from God and is by faith.

In this passage Paul speaks to us about this subject of pride in oneself. He starts off by telling us pride is a form of confidence one can have in oneself, and he knew he had more to be proud of than others around him. He was a Jew from the tribe of Benjamin, a Hebrew of Hebrews; in regard to the law, a Pharisee. As for his zeal, he was to the point of persecuting the Christian Church, and for legalistic righteousness, he was faultless.

But he then tells us how everything he had considered to be

responsible for his profit, he now considers as loss for the sake of Christ. He goes further to say everything is a loss compared to the greatness of knowing Christ Jesus. He considers all of his personal advantages as rubbish, so he may gain Christ. He tells us the only righteousness to be found comes from God and is by faith alone. This is the testimony of a man who had every advantage one could have in his time. He admits to having a sense of pride in himself so strong, he would put to death others who lived contrary to his beliefs. But upon his conversion into Christianity, he left all such feelings behind. This is our example. We need only to follow.

Another passage Paul was inspired to write for us is found in 1 Corinthians 13:11; "When I was a child, I talked like a child, I thought like a child, I reasoned like a child. When I became a man, I put childish ways behind me." This passage relates to any prideful condition instilled in us during our childhood. It is not the way a man of God will think; he will ask God to help remove such thinking from his mind because all believers are told to do the same as Paul.

So, for you who call yourselves believers, and yet you still believe there is something in you inherently better than some others, you have been duped. You are guilty of pride leading to prejudicial thoughts, and you must rid yourselves of this nature. It does not matter if your parents, or anybody else, placed this sense of superiority in you; you are responsible for your own behavior now. You are not just a child now; you are a child of God. We are sons and daughters of the Lord, and are held to His standard, and we must strive to reach that standard.

I offer you the encouragement coming from the example Paul set before us. His journey from pride is something we can all take to heart. Let it serve as proof there are none of us who are so deeply rooted in our pride we cannot overcome it. For further assurance you can overcome, turn to Mark 10:27; "Jesus looked at them and said, 'With man this is impossible, but not with God; all things are possible with God.'" Our Lord Jesus states everything is possible for those who believe. Although with man something may be impossible to achieve, with God all things are possible! Although you may feel it is impossible for you to do away with this spirit of prejudice, it is not when God is on your side. Ask the Holy Spirit to guide you in the journey, and He will do so. Just follow His teaching and you will reach your goals.

There is no prefix attached to the Christian believer anywhere in the Word of God. What I mean is you will not find any verses calling someone out as a particular class of believer; there are simply believers and non-believers. God does not use a prefix denoting race or gender, age or occupation, or any other trait as a method of separating classes of believers. You will not find terms such as White-Christian, Intelligent-Christian, or for that matter, Baptist or Methodist, Catholic or Lutheran, or any others. These terms do not exist, as our God did not place them in His Word.

When we do overcome our past, the right thing to do is to try to rectify the wrong we have done to others. To be sure, there will be some who will not forgive us for our past behavior, but God will. He will see we have tried to make amends with the ones we have transgressed, and we are told He will look upon us with favor when we do this. He knows us as we really are on the inside. He sees what is in our hearts. He will be pleased with our efforts when they are meant to glorify Him through our actions.

Returning now to our title of unworthiness, it doesn't really matter what causes you to feel this condition. Whether it's because of some bad thing you have done, or some physical trait you believe makes you inferior, or because of things people have said about you; it really doesn't matter.

You have read passages from God's Word in this chapter proving all those thoughts are lies. We read about how God loved us so much He sent His Son to die in our place on the Cross. God wouldn't ask His Son to do that for people He thought were worthless. Your feelings of unworthiness can actually help you as you seek God, because everybody is unworthy of God's grace.

Knowing you are unworthy is one of the first steps in realizing your need for God, so it is something to rejoice over! Now you just need to talk to God from your heart and let Him know your need for His grace and love. That's what salvation is all about: just reaching the point of realizing there is nothing in this world to satisfy the needs in your heart. Only God can supply what we are lacking in our lives.

So talk to God, and tell Him about the pain in your heart. Tell Him how you want to become one of His children. He will listen, He will adopt you into His family, and your pain will finally go away. There will still be sad times, but God will always be there to comfort you. So do it today, don't put it off any longer! Just let your heart tell you what to say, and God will do the rest!

Chapter Five

It's Not Politically Correct

This term is certainly one we are all very much aware of in today's society. You can't avoid hearing it if you watch the news on television or read any newspaper. This state of political correctness people refer to means different things to different people, and some of you will define it differently than I do. As you read my observations on political correctness and its meaning, I ask you to tolerate any differences you may find between your understanding of its definition and my own.

In general, I see political correctness as a state of trying to not offend any group or collection of individuals having some common association between them. This common thread could be something political, it can be a sexual orientation, it can be gender related, or it could be race related. Basically, it can be just about anything a group calls out as an identifiable characteristic of their collective unit. The central theme of political correctness lies in the requirement of remaining inoffensive in any way towards any particular group.

When observing the real world, and how this political correctness is truly being carried out, I have noticed it is only the group of people who call themselves Christian seeming to be exempt from this policy. If you pay any attention to the news, there are cases daily, highlighting people who are actively attacking Christian principles in an offensive manner. However, they are not chastised for being politically incorrect; they are actually being supported as being on the side of right. If you disagree with my observation of this fact, I urge you to pay closer attention to the way the media showcases examples of challenges made to Christian values and doctrine.

Try keeping a sort of score card, and record each time you hear or read a story dealing with Christian values—whether negative or positive in the way it is presented. It won't take very long for you to determine which way the trend is flowing, I guarantee it.

One good example of this is the obvious attempt to remove God's name from our Pledge of Allegiance, from our currency, from our schools, from our governmental buildings, and basically from every facet where His name is still represented in our country. There is no outcry over the way these activities are held as being so offensive towards the Christian community. It is the exact opposite we find. The politically correct community endorses these activities and supports them wholeheartedly. We Christians must endure this hardship, and we should be praying for our nation to turn from this path we are rushing down headlong towards the destruction of the Christian principles our founding fathers relied on when establishing this nation.

God's Word speaks on this very subject in the book of Psalm 33:12; "Blessed is the nation whose God is the Lord, the people he chose for His inheritance." When we look back at our nation's history from the time when our forefathers established our government based on God's principles, we see we have been blessed. Now that we are removing those principles from public life, the blessings have become few and far between.

For the nation which chooses to not follow God's laws, a warning is given in Isaiah 60:12; "For the nation or kingdom that will not serve you will perish; it will be utterly ruined." It is because of these promises and warnings given to us in God's Word that Christian believers must pray without end for the sake of our country. Those of us who are trying to live righteously can make a difference in the way God either blesses or curses this nation, and we must do whatever we can to help steer this country back towards the godly principles on which it was founded.

The politically correct have applied this ideology in a self-serving manner, and limited how we can represent God to others. It has become an excuse for rejecting Christianity, and was mentioned by several people I spoke with. Several different situations people have transferred this concept onto will be mentioned here, and the error of their reasoning will be exposed through God's Word. As we look at these instances, I believe we will find that although the title of political correctness is a fairly new one, the situations it is being applied to have nothing new about them.

This politically correct crowd is trying to place God Himself under their guidelines, and this is causing a lot of misconceptions such as: if God loves us, He could never punish us. Many people feel it is an oxymoron to even suggest someone who loves you would still be able to punish you just for being human. God has said much about the love He has for us, and He has also said much about the punishment He will deliver for our rebellious acts. There are many Scriptures written on both of these subjects, which should be an indication of their significance to God.

Concerning God's love for the world, a familiar verse is John 3:16-17; "For God so loved the world that he gave his one and only Son, that whosoever believes in him shall not perish but have eternal life. For God did not send his Son into the world to condemn the world, but that through him the world might be saved." This is a passage you may have seen on a poster at a sporting event, on a billboard along the roadside, or perhaps on a t-shirt that someone was wearing. It is probably one of the most familiar texts from the Bible, but have you truly thought about the message contained there in those verses?

God so loved the world that He gave His Son. God did not loan Jesus to us, He gave Him to us. Christ was sent into this world to lead us into salvation through His death on the Cross. God has said our sin must be punished, and Jesus came to bear the punishment for us so we could re-establish a relationship with God. We had sinned, which is rebellion against God. So because of our rebellion, we had become separated from God. God sent Jesus into this world to bridge the gap we had created through our sinful rebellion.

Jesus tells us who He is in John 14:6; "I am the way, the truth and the life, no one comes to the Father except through me." He is the only one who can help us to have fellowship with God; there is no other way or any other person we can go through to find God.

What an example of unselfish love God showed us through the sacrificing of His own Son! He placed our inequities upon Jesus, and He died for our transgressions; even though He

Himself was without sin! Our Father in Heaven showed us this immeasurable love, and His Son showed unfaltering obedience to His Father's will. Taken together, this shows us what is meant by unconditional love. This love is exclaimed for us in 1 John 3:1; "How great is the love the Father has lavished on us, that we should be called children of God! And that is what we are! The reason the world does not know us is that it did not know him." God's Word has shown us the way to become His children through believing in His Son, and the sacrifice He paid for us on the Cross.

Another example of God's love is found in Romans 5:8; "But God demonstrates His own love for us in this: While we were yet sinners, Christ died for us." Oh the love running throughout God's Word! The theme is there for all to see! It's easy to understand why so many of us concentrate our attention on this amazing love God has shown for mankind. It is hard not to. However, a problem arises when churches focus all of their attention on this love, and ignore the fact that God has also promised punishment for those who continue in rebellion and refuse His gift of eternal life through Jesus Christ.

This is a result of churches trying to become "seeker friendly," in a political kind of way, and not preaching anything from the Scriptures if it might offend the non-believers attending their church services. This is how the attempt to be politically correct is doing damage in our Christian community. People who may be looking for answers to the problems unraveling their lives may only be hearing how God loves them no matter what they do. They are being taught God is only a God of love, and are not being told the rest from God's Word because it may offend them.

It is easy to use the Scriptures to reinforce this teaching

that our God is a God of love, because there are so many references telling us this is true. But if we will only use the same standard regarding his wrath, there are twice as many verses telling us about God's hatred of sin and the punishment He has sworn to administer to those who are guilty of sinful rebellion against Him.

Any church choosing to neglect preaching this fact to its attendees is doing them a terrible injustice. We all need to know the absolute truth our God has laid down for us in His Word. In many believers' lives, it was the knowledge of the eternal punishment promised to the unforgiven sinner that was responsible in leading them to their acceptance of the Gospel message. Anyone called to share God's message must share it completely, and we are told this very thing in Deuteronomy 12:32; "See that you do all I command you; do not add to it or take away from it." We are also told in Revelations 22:18–19:

> I warn everyone who hears the words of the prophecy of this book: If anyone adds anything to them, God will add to him the plagues described in this book. And if anyone takes words away from this book of prophecy, God will take away from him his share in the tree of life and in the holy city, which are described in this book.

So, not only are we told we must share all of the words found in the Scriptures, we are warned of punishment if we do not. God does not care whether or not men find Him to be politically incorrect; He is not dictated by the whims of men. This whole concept of political correctness is proving itself to be just one more way for man to justify his own sinful behavior. Although man tries to change the packaging and alter the perception of others towards his behavior, sin is still sin and those that are unrepentant will be punished just as God has said.

Another passage sharing this warning is found in the book of Isaiah 13:11, 13:

> I will punish the world for its evil, the wicked for their sins. I will put an end to the arrogance of the haughty and will humble the pride of the ruthless...Therefore I will make the heavens tremble; and the earth will shake from its place at the wrath of the Lord Almighty, in the day of His burning anger.

God has clearly stated what He is going to do with the earth and the wicked sinners on the day of His wrath. This does not mean He stops loving us. It just means that because He is a just God, He must punish those who have rejected the covering of sins through Christ.

As born-again believers, we have accepted the Bible as the infallible Word of God. Therefore, we must believe a day is coming when God's wrath is going to be poured out upon the world and those who are living in rebellion against Him. I do not understand someone's reluctance to preach this knowledge to those who need to hear it. They are entitled to hear it, and we are told to preach it. If someone is offended by this preaching, what of it?! Perhaps it is through this teaching they will finally find their own need for forgiveness, and repent of their sins!

It is our duty to tell others about the truths found in the Bible. If we don't, then how will they hear them? God's Word says this very thing in Romans 10:14; "How, then, can they call on the one they have not believed in? And how can they believe in the one of whom they have not heard? And how can they hear without someone preaching to them?"

It is exactly because we don't want others to fall into punishment that we should be lead to share the warnings from God like this one from 2 Thessalonians 1:8–9; "He will punish those who do not know God and do not obey the gospel of our Lord Jesus. They will be punished with everlasting destruction and shut out from the presence of the Lord and from the majesty of His power."

We must tell people that God will sentence them to eternal destruction and separation from Him if they do not accept and receive the gift of salvation. If we only preach the message of love, but omit the consequences of unbelief, we lessen the chances for people to come to Christ. The Scripture we read from the book of Revelation was warning us that we must not hold back anything written in the Scriptures. God put everything there because it is an integral part of the message that will help people to see why they need Him and why they should be saved.

When someone preaches the message of saving grace, what good is it if there is nothing to be saved from? It is foolish to tell somebody they need to be saved, but then to omit the mentioning of what will happen to them if they are not. This is where the politically correct attitude leads to much confusion. If all you hear at a church is how everything is wrapped in love, how can you believe there is a punishment in hell reserved for sinners? Even though different denominations are using the same Bible, some are only preaching part of the salvation message. This in itself is very harmful, but some take it further and pronounce judgment on those who preach the whole message as being mean-spirited, or as the topic in question calls it: politically incorrect.

Many verses in God's Word share both the promise of salvation, and the warning for those who don't receive God's gift, in the same passage. One example of this is found in John 3:36; "Whoever believes in the Son has eternal life, but whoever rejects the Son will not see life, for God's wrath remains on him." How much more specific could God have been in defining for us exactly who is going to suffer from His wrath? God did not only promise us eternal life for believing, He promised us His wrath if we do not. I have seen advertising on a church billboard promising, "You won't find fire and brimstone in our messages." What a shame for a church to say such a thing, when our Bible tells us we are to share all that is written down there. How can we reason amongst ourselves to eliminate part of God's message from our ministries simply for the sake of being politically correct?

If you find yourself in a church following this guideline of being inoffensive towards those attending, then I urge you to seek out a different church that preaches the whole Word of God. Do so as quickly as you can. Your very soul depends on it! But even more important, read the Bible for yourself. God's Word is worth more than you can imagine, so read it!

There are many verses telling us exactly how valuable God's Word really is, and one of them is Romans 15:4. It says, "For everything that was written in the past was written to teach us, so that through endurance and the encouragement of the Scriptures we might have hope." Another similar verse, Revelations 1:3, says "Blessed is the one who reads the words of this prophecy, and blessed are those who hear it and take to heart what is written in it, because the time is near." As you read the Word, what you need to do is pray for God to help you do that: take it to heart.

Another verse touching on this subject is found in Isaiah 55:11; "So is my word that goes out from my mouth; It will not return to me empty, but will accomplish what I desire and achieve the purpose for which I sent it." God's word involves both love and punishment; it is not one without the other. Do not waste your time here on earth trying to be politically correct, instead, live it being Biblically correct. Then you can help others see the love coming from the gift of eternal life God offers to us through His Son's death on the Cross, while also helping others to see the punishment for those who reject His gift.

There are many people out there searching for a relationship with God, but they are only human. It makes perfect sense when we think about the reasons why people would be happy to find a place, calling itself a Christian church, which goes out of its way to make sure their preaching ministry never offends its congregation. We can all see how enjoyable of an experience that must be for everybody present. To feel one is right with God, or be told that even if you're not, He will forgive you because He is a God of love, will naturally make anybody feel contentment. But we have seen from Scripture, it is a false sense of contentment. It is not what our Bible teaches.

Many of us have seen the problem with individuals living lifestyles contrary to God's written Word, who are attending one of these so-called "liberal churches." These "liberal" churches may either water down the warning messages from Scripture, or ignore them all together. For the sake of those who may be attending this type of church, I want to share what God's Word has to say. I am well aware of the fact this will qualify myself for the title of narrow-minded, right-wing, radically conservative type of Christian, but I am commanded by Scripture to teach what is there.

The command to teach in this way is found in 2 Timothy 4:2–5:

> Preach the Word; be prepared in season and out of season; correct, rebuke and encourage—with great patience and careful instruction. For the time will come when men will not put up with sound doctrine. Instead, to suit their own desires, they will gather around them a great number of teachers to say what their itching ears want to hear. They will turn their ears away from the truth and turn aside to myths. But you, keep your head in all situations, endure hardship, do the work of an evangelist, discharge all the duties of your ministry.

The reason we are to teach God's Word in full is because when we do, some who hear may turn away from a lifestyle that is sinful. This is the objective we should all be striving for, because there is nothing to compare to the euphoria felt from someone's conversion into Christianity. Even the angels in Heaven rejoice, for they have joined the ranks of the forgiven believers: the children of God!

Choosing one area in today's society is very easy. Let's look at what God says to couples who want to live together without the benefit of marriage. This is so commonplace in our day and age, it goes largely without notice. Secular society has endorsed this practice completely and without question. It has given "living together" its blessing. There are countless authors, media personalities, and psychologists adding their weight to the acceptance of this practice. Mankind has been rebellious against the laws of God since he was created, and we are definitely not changing yet. This area of "living together" is just one more example of our defiance.

As believers, we find ourselves suffering the worst possible damage when couples live this type of sinful lifestyle while professing to be Christians. What makes matters worse is how these couples attend a church which refuses to teach on this area of sin. Worse yet, they may offer up some sense of approval for it. This approval may simply be in the form of silent head nodding over the incidences of cohabitation. It may be in the form of dismissing it as modern behavior, or it may just be dismissed as being part of loving each other. It does not matter whether the acceptance is through active allowance of the behavior or passively ignoring it; both are wrong according to the Scriptures.

God says in the book of Hebrews 13:4; "Marriage should be honored by all, and the marriage bed kept pure, for God will judge the adulterer and all the sexually immoral." This is exactly what every Christian church should be teaching all of its members whether they participate in activity God has called sexually immoral or not. It is the duty of the church to tell you God will judge you for this type of behavior, and He has said you will be punished for it. If your church "looks the other way" about such behavior in any way, move on and find one that does not.

Speaking to any Christian-professing individuals involved in this type of sexual activity, I urge you to read from 1 John 3:4–6; "Everyone who sins breaks the law; in fact, sin is lawlessness. But you know that he appeared so that he might take away our sins, and in him is no sin. No one who lives in him keeps on sinning. No one who continues to sin has either seen him or known him."

The apostle John was not trying to tell us Christians would

live their lives without sin, but he was saying we would not live sinful lives. This means although believers will still sin by giving in to the desires of the flesh, they will be convicted of their sins. This conviction, which comes from the Holy Spirit, leads to repentance and forgiveness. Then we move forward and stop habitually committing that particular sin; it will not become the pattern for our life.

Jesus taught this same principle when he faced a woman caught in the act of adultery. The people were demanding her to be stoned, in accordance with their law. We find Jesus' response in John 8:3–11:

> The teachers of the law and the Pharisees brought in a woman caught in adultery. They made her stand before the group and said to Jesus, "Teacher, this woman was caught in the act of adultery. In the Law Moses commanded us to stone such women. Now what do you say?" They were using this question as a trap, in order to have a basis for accusing him.
>
> But Jesus bent down and started to write on the ground with his finger. When they kept questioning him, he straightened up and said to them, "If any one of you is without sin, let him be the first to throw a stone at her." Again he stooped down and wrote on the ground.
>
> At this, those who heard began to go away one at a time, the older ones first, until only Jesus was left, with the woman still standing there. Jesus straightened up and asked her, "Woman, where are they? Has no one condemned you?"

"No one, sir," she said.

"Then neither do I condemn you," Jesus declared. "Go now and leave your life of sin."

Your need to leave your life of sin is what your church should be preaching to you, just like Jesus taught this woman caught in the act of adultery. If it's not, there are many churches out there that are preaching the whole Word of God. If you visit different churches and pray for God to show you which one is right for you, I promise you will be lead to a church fulfilling its role according to God's Word.

Another lifestyle many of the "liberal" churches are choosing to either endorse or give a pass to is the homosexual one. We are all aware of how much effort Hollywood has put into legitimizing this type of behavior. Science has thrown its weight into the battle by claiming to have found a genetic trait leading to this sexual orientation. Some researchers have even published findings making that claim. The media became energized about this new discovery, and it was in every paper and on every news program aired on television. However, a short time later when other scientists pointed out the flaws in the studies concluding this result, the media failed to put the same effort into announcing their findings.

Just like any other issue we want to understand according to God's Word, all we have to do is turn to the Scriptures. Homosexuality is no different than any other issue from life; everything is addressed in God's Word if we just read it. What God says about this one can be found in 1 Corinthians 6:9–11:

Do you not know that the wicked will not inherit

> the kingdom of God? Do not be deceived: Neither the sexually immoral nor idolaters nor adulterers nor male prostitutes nor homosexual offenders nor thieves nor the greedy nor drunkards nor slanderers nor swindlers will inherit the kingdom of God. And this is what some of you were. But you were washed, you were sanctified, you were justified in the name of the Lord Jesus Christ and by the Spirit of our God.

It is important to note the many types of sinful behaviors mentioned. It's even more important to realize the Apostle Paul was teaching Christians when he preached this message. Some believers used to live their lives in those sinful manners listed, including the offense of homosexual sin. But they no longer are living as they were. They have been washed and sanctified by the blood of Christ! Paul applauds the fact they no longer live the sinful lives they did before their salvation.

As Christians, we are told to leave our sinful lives behind us in God's Word. Do not let anyone tell you homosexuality is acceptable to God; if you read your Bible you will know it is not. But do not let anyone tell you the homosexual life-style is somehow worse than any of the others Paul mentioned in that passage of Scriptures either; it is not. They are all equally sinful in the eyes of God. There will not be a higher level of rejoicing in Heaven for one saved from this life behavior than there will be for one who is saved from a life of lying and slandering. All of these traits are sinful. All of them require conviction and repentance in order to receive forgiveness. These types of rebellion are just examples of sin, and this is what your church should be preaching to you.

Another way people try to place God under the guidelines of political correctness is in the way God is blamed for the unfortunate, evil things that go on every day. Now they may not actually say God makes these things happen, but the fact He doesn't stop them from happening is their problem. It can be almost any type of bad occurrence in someone's life, which causes them to place this blame on God. The end result is the development of a great anger towards God.

In our society, many people say if there really were a God, He would not let bad things happen to us. The other side to this way of thinking says God is the one who actually does the bad things to us. These views are mistaken, and when believed, they will cause anger towards God. It is a sad state for any to find themselves in, and it is also a dangerous one. It is not hard to understand how this feeling comes about in people as they enter into times of suffering and tribulation, but there is no excusing it in the life of a believer.

There are many trials that can lead to this feeling of anger towards God. Some obvious examples are ones like an illness that strikes us or someone we hold dear. It may be the illness is very painful and debilitating, or perhaps it may lead to the death of someone we love. Another example can be just watching all of the horrendous things happening in our world and showing up in our newspapers and television broadcasts every day. This is something we have a never-ending supply of because evil things happen in our world on a daily basis. Financial misdealing is another area people have trouble with, and God is sometimes blamed for their failures to manage their finances, leading to still more anger.

When it comes to blaming God, we are all too quick to do so. After we have admitted we all sometimes feel anger towards God, we need to turn to God's Word to learn how to deal with this problem. As I have said before, this is the first place to look every time. We can do no better than to turn to

God's Word for our answers, so I urge you to do so whenever you find yourself with questions in life.

A good place to read about this "blaming God" syndrome is the book of Job. For those not familiar with him, he was a righteous man, a wealthy man, and a man who had most everything his heart desired. There was nothing he lacked. As we say in our modern society, he had it all.

We can see how special Job was in the book of Job 1:8; "Then the Lord said to Satan, 'Have you considered my servant Job? There is no one on earth like him; he is blameless and upright, a man who fears God and shuns evil.'" Satan had come to visit God, and told God he had been traveling throughout the earth. God asked him if he had noticed what a good man Job was. Satan replied by saying the only reason Job was good was because God had protected him by putting a hedge around him and allowing no harm to strike him. God's response was to tell satan he could strike all belongings of Job's, but not touch the man himself. In today's terminology, we would say God told satan to "give it his best shot."

Satan went out from the presence of the Lord, and the result of his horrible attack upon Job can be found in Job 1:14–19:

> A messenger came to Job and said, "The oxen were plowing and the donkeys were grazing nearby, and the Sabeans attacked and carried them off. They put the servants to the sword, and I alone have escaped to tell you!"
>
> While he was still speaking, another messenger came and said, "The fire of God fell from the sky and burned

> up the sheep and the servants, I alone escaped to tell you!"
>
> While he was still speaking, another messenger came and said, "The Chaldeans formed three raiding parties and swept down on your camels and carried them off. They put the servants to the sword, and I alone escaped to tell you!"
>
> While he was still speaking, yet another messenger came and said, "Your sons and daughters were feasting and drinking wine at the oldest brother's house, when suddenly a mighty wind swept in from the desert and struck the four corners of the house. It collapsed on them and they are dead, and I am the only one who escaped to tell you!"

It is hard to imagine the losses Job suffered at one time in this passage of Scripture. He was informed how all of the enormous wealth he owned in livestock was taken away from him, his servants had been killed, and his sons and daughters all died in a terrible storm. The total loss of our financial assets would cause much grief on its own, but the loss of so many loved ones would be unbearable!

Remember, the Lord had singled out Job because there was no one else like him. He was more righteous than any others in the world, which is why he was used as an example for us to follow. We find his reaction in Job 1:20–22:

> At this, Job got up and tore his robe and shaved his head. Then he fell to the ground in worship and said: "Naked I came from my mother's womb, and naked

> I will depart. The Lord gave and the Lord has taken away; may the name of the Lord be praised." In all this, Job did not sin by charging God with wrongdoing.

Who else would be able to respond in this manner? It would be a rare man who could behave like that. In all of this turmoil, Job still gave God credit for all he had before calamity struck him. With the help of the Holy Spirit, we too can respond in a similar fashion when struck with the unimaginable. The bigger the strife, the more we must rely on His guidance. Not only did Job still praise God; he would not charge Him with wrongdoing, and we are told if he did, it would have been sin on his part!

You might think satan would be satisfied with the righteousness of Job, but he wasn't. He went to see God again, and God asked him if he had considered his servant Job. The Lord pointed out again how Job was still honoring Him. Satan snapped back about how Job was like that only because He had spared his own flesh and bone. Satan argued that if he could strike Job, he would curse God to His face.

The result of this conversation is found in Job 2:6–10:

> The Lord said to satan, 'Very well, then, he is in your hands; but you must spare his life.' So satan departed and afflicted Job with painful sores from the soles of his feet to the top of his head. Then Job took a piece of broken pottery and scraped himself with it as he sat among the ashes. His wife said to him, 'Are you still holding on to your integrity? Curse God and die!' He replied, 'You are talking like a foolish woman. Shall we accept good from God, and not trouble?' In all this, Job did not sin in what he said.

Now Job was suffering physically. His body was in great pain, adding to his misery from the previous trials he had endured. What mental anguish he suffered through, and he still refused to sin by saying something wrong about his God. Even his own wife urged him to curse his God. But Job scolded her, and refused to give in. I am sure his wife loved him, and she did not mean to push him into sin. I believe she felt such pity for him, and was so emotional over everything happening to them, she just lost her control.

This example of Job's suffering is greater than anything we could imagine in most lives. I hate to think anybody could be put through more of an ordeal than Job was. But Job was not finished yet. He was to be tempted even further through the misguided efforts of three of his closest friends: Eliphaz, Bildad, and Zophar.

These three came to see Job when they heard of his great tragedies, just like our friends come to see us when bad things happen to us. When they arrived, they just sat in silence with him. They mourned with him for all the losses he had endured, and continued in silence for a whole week! This alone may have been enough for Job; his closest friends joining him in his pain. But they moved on from this phase and tried to reason with him about the causes for all of his troubles.

To get the whole message passed back and forth between Job and his friends, you must read the book. In condensed form, they ended up telling him he must have done some horrible thing which lead to God's hand being against him. When I read how they tried to counsel Job, I believe they were just like his wife had been earlier; they talked out of love for him, but their advice was not sound. They were wrong to think nothing this bad could happen to a man who was good.

Their mistake was believing bad things only happen to bad people. This is not the case. Satan attacks all the righteous people he can

Job listened to all he could take, and answered them in Job 27: 2–6:

> As surely as God lives, who has denied me justice, the Almighty, who has made me taste bitterness of soul, as long as I have life within me, the breath of God in my nostrils, my lips will not speak wickedness, and my tongue will utter no deceit. I will never admit you are in the right; till I die, I will not deny my integrity. I will maintain my righteousness and never let go of it; my conscience will not reproach me as long as I live.

Job has finally broken down and says God has denied him justice and made him taste bitterness of soul. After the prodding of his friends, he finally gave in to a spirit of disgust. He claimed his integrity, but he moved to the point of saying God was unfair. After Job said this, a young man by the name of Elihu stepped forward to share what he thought.

He was a younger man, so he waited to speak until his elders finished what they had to say. We hear from him in Job 32: 6–9:

> So Elihu son of Barakel the Buzite said, "I am young in years, and you are old; that is why I was fearful, not daring to tell you what I know. I thought, 'Age should speak; advanced years should teach wisdom.' But it is the spirit in a man, the breath of the Almighty, that gives him understanding. It is not only the old who are wise, not only the aged who understand what is

right."

Elihu was angry with Job for justifying his own integrity rather than God's. He continues in Job 34:10–12; "So listen to me you men of understanding. Far be it from God to do evil, from the Almighty to do wrong. He repays a man for what he has done; he brings upon him what his conduct deserves. It is unthinkable that God would do wrong, that the Almighty would pervert justice." He said these things because of Job's justifying himself, rather than justifying the Lord. Elihu shows us we do not have to be old to have wisdom given by God. This is a fact we should all remember, because sometimes the young may be given the wisdom their elders need to hear.

After Elihu had spoken, the Lord spoke to Job from out of a storm. Part of what God said is found in Job 38:4–11:

> Where were you when I laid the earth's foundation? Tell me, if you understand. Who marked off its dimensions? Surely you know! Who stretched a measuring line across it? On what were its footings set, or who laid its cornerstone—while the morning stars sang together and all the angels shouted for joy? Who shut up the sea behind doors when it burst forth from the womb, when I made the clouds its garment and wrapped it in thick darkness, when I fixed limits for it and set its doors and bars in place, when I said, "This far you may come and no farther; here is where your proud waves halt"?

Job was reminded by the Lord of who he was calling unjust. By simply stating a few parts of His works of Creation, God had reminded Job of the unimaginable wisdom and power He has. This is how Job erred; he forgot the sovereignty of God!

So many of us make the same mistake when hit by the plagues of life. Illnesses in loved ones or in ourselves; financial losses leaving us devastated; personal relationships going wrong, such as divorces and separations; tragic events taking place such as the terrorist attacks on civilians; the list is never-ending! On the other end of this spectrum, we should include those things we desire in our lives, but are not granted. People desire personal relationships not materializing. They want job promotions and other means of gaining wealth; whatever it is they desire, they tend to blame God when it doesn't happen.

When we blame God for our misfortunes and say things like, "It isn't fair," we are forgetting, just like Job, that God is sovereign. Job was a man who forgot, and he was sorry for his mistake. We can find his apology to God in Job 40:3–5; "Then Job answered the Lord: I am unworthy—how can I reply to you? I put my hand over my mouth. I spoke once, but I have no answer—twice, but I will say no more." Job acknowledges he had no right to question God's actions in any way, and we should do the same.

This does not mean we will not have questions about things, it simply means we can't sit as judges on whether or not God is just and fair. We do not know what God knows. We were not there in the beginning, and we do not know the whole plan God worked out for this world. So if you ever feel like venting at God, a great passage to read is from Ecclesiastes 5:2; "Do not be quick with your mouth, do not be hasty in your heart to utter anything before God. God is in Heaven, and you are on earth, so let your words be few."

As we travel through our lives, we will suffer trials and tribulations. But we are told we should count these trials as good for us; they are meant to build us up as we overcome them. One place we see this is in Psalm 119:65–68; "Do good to your servant according to your word, O Lord. Teach me knowledge and good judgment, for I believe your commands. Before I was afflicted I went astray, but now I obey your word. You are good, and what you do is good; teach me your decrees."

Another good example can be found in Philippians 4:11b–13:

> I have learned to be content whatever the circumstances. I know what it is to be in need, and I know what it is to have plenty. I have learned the secret of being content in any and every situation, whether well fed or hungry, whether living in plenty or in want. I can do everything through Him who gives me strength.

This passage really sums up being thankful for what you have.

Still one more passage of Scripture we should look at tells to remember that no matter what we are struggling with, God is behind everything that ever was, is, or will be. Romans 8:28 says; "And we know that in all things God works for the good of those who love him, who have been called according to his purpose." Though it will be difficult, we must remember even the bad things are working together for the good of those who love God.

I hope you have seen in these passages of Scripture that we have no right to be angry towards God. I hope you will be able to overcome the tendency to get angry when trials come. I want you to know you are not alone; we all have times we must fight this condition. Lean on your brothers and sisters in

Christ. They will help you to overcome, just as you must help them to do the same.

The last area falling under this category of political correctness is the concept saying we should let everyone believe what they want to believe, and leave them to their own understanding. I have had people use this line when I tried to witness to them, and I struggle to overcome this barrier. It's not easy climbing this fence, but we are told we must try to do so.

Jesus said in Mark 16:15, "Go into all the world and preach the good news to all creation." Another passage like this one is found in 2 Timothy 4:2; "Preach the Word; be prepared in season and out of season; correct, rebuke and encourage—with great patience and careful instruction."

I only used two passages, but there are many more if you need encouragement in this area. No matter how often someone says we should just "leave them alone," when it comes to witnessing, you are commanded by our Lord to witness to all people throughout the world. We must make an honest attempt at serving this commission given to us. The stakes are too high to do any less for those we come into contact with, for the stakes are their very souls.

So heed the call and obey the Lord's command. Don't stop because people say you are politically incorrect for bothering someone. I am not advocating any witnessing considered obnoxious in nature, but simply saying we must share the Good News about Jesus Christ and God's plan of salvation! Remember to do as instructed in Ephesians 4:15; "Instead, speaking the truth in love, we will in all things grow up into him who is the Head, that is, Christ." We must strive to always tell the truth, and to do so in love. If we concentrate on truth only, without love, we will appear as harsh taskmasters. If we speak only out of love, and leave truth out, we create a mushy misrepresentation of God's laws. So do as we are told, speak the truth in love, and you cannot go wrong.

We are told to obey those placed in authority over us, and we must do so. But we need to participate in determining who those individuals will be, such as in our right to vote in democratic elections. We should vote for leaders who acknowledge our Lord's kingdom. But remember, as I quoted from the book of Philippians 4:11, "Be content whatever the circumstances." We are to press on regardless of the situations we find ourselves in, no matter how politically incorrect others find us to be.

We can never go wrong if we remember God is always correct, always truthful, always loving, and always there for us. No matter what the trials we face, we need to remember what He said in Deuteronomy 31:6; "Be strong and courageous. Do not be afraid or terrified because of them, for the Lord your God goes with you; He will never leave you nor forsake you."

This applies to any challenge we face in our walk, do not be afraid, God is with you. As I said earlier, do not strive to be politically correct, strive instead to be Biblically correct. If you do so in truth and love, you are doing as God instructed. No matter what alternative may be presented to you, there is nothing comparing to the way God tells us to live; just trust and obey Him.

Chapter Six

I Don't Need a Crutch to Lean On

No Crutch Needed

The heading for this sixth chapter comes from my youngest son, Benjamin. He brought it to my attention during a conversation we had about the different reasons he has heard people use for dismissing Christianity. Although he travels in the twenty-something crowd, the excuses these young people offer are much the same as every other age group I have encountered. My son stated that whenever his friends ask him about what his father is, he tells them I am a Christian. The title of this chapter is their direct response, "It's nice to have a crutch if you need one."

Using Webster's once more, we can find the definition of the word "crutch." Webster's defines it as, "A support typically fitted for under the armpit for use by those disabled or unable to walk under their own efforts." I like this definition, and I believe it fits perfectly into the general scheme those making this comment have in their minds. They are referring to the fact that they believe we who follow Christ do so because we are unable to navigate through this world on our own. It's ironic, but I agree with them in principle. However, there is a huge difference in the way I see this condition, and the way they do.

Looking at the way these young people express this concept, they are thinking in terms of their belief in the strength of their youth. They believe they are capable of anything they set their minds to, and that they have the energy within them necessary to accomplish whatever it is they decide to tackle. I remember my way of thinking being the same at that age; however, sharing this similarity with young people is a waste of time because it doesn't do anything to change their attitudes. They might still allow you to relate to them into your early thirties, but as you close in on your fifties, your chances are very slim. When you talk with these young people, they do not look at you as someone who used to be young, they simply see you as someone old.

One of the worst mistakes we can make is when we view these young people as children. We need to see them for what they are: young men and women. Teenagers should be treated in the same way as these young adults, because once they quit being children, they become young adults. Reaching these younger adults is of the utmost importance. If we approach this group of young adults with the attitude that they are not capable of making mature decisions, we are doing them a terrible injustice. In order to have any chance of success when reaching out and witnessing to them, we must tell them that God views us as equals. We need to tell them that just being older does not give us some kind of advantage with God. Try to make sure they understand that fact.

It is only after clearing this mental hurdle that you can begin to have any success when witnessing to this age group. Then you simply follow the guidelines God has set forth for us in His Word. This first step is always the same—turn to the Scriptures. Most young people believe they know everything. When witnessing to them, we have to realize that they feel the older generation knows nothing about life pertaining to their generation. This is a fact of youth, and if we are honest, it's easy to admit how most, if not all, of us felt the same way at times during our own youth.

Society has called this phenomenon the "generation gap." As far as I can tell, it has existed for as long as there have been parents and children. If you are from an older generation, can you still remember what it was like to believe in your own strength? I can still recall feeling invincible as a young adult, can't you? I remember what it was like to believe you were right about everything; and nobody could tell you otherwise. If someone did try, you simply dismissed them as being irrelevant to your own circumstances. As I reminisce about the passions we all have felt during our youth, I find myself believing I am not as old as I sometimes feel. I believe part of the flame from our youth is still burning inside of us, and it should be just enough to reach those who are all aflame in their youth. Society has an expression covering the way I'm talking about; "you're only as old as you feel." So when we reach out to young people, let's all try to feel a little younger than maybe we are, so they have a better chance of listening to us.

Following through on the belief that young adults have the same capacity to understand as those who are not so young, let's look at what God's Word says about these youthful beliefs in self-sufficiency. A majority of my selections will come from Solomon's book of Proverbs, as his wisdom on this area surpasses anyone else's that I have ever encountered. The first such wisdom can be found in Proverbs 3:5–7; "Trust in the Lord with all your heart and lean not on your own understanding; in all your ways acknowledge him, and he will make your paths straight. Do not be wise in your own eyes; fear the Lord and shun evil."

In this passage, God is not telling us to use Him as a crutch. Neither does He say we do not have the capacity to understand. He says we should lean on Him in order to achieve the highest level of understanding. In order to reach our highest level of understanding, all we have to do is trust in the Lord with all our heart. We are even promised a reward for doing so; He will make our paths straight. Think about how valuable such a promise is, and how much easier it would be to travel through life if we could avoid many of the twists and turns we run into? When thinking about this passage, do not make the mistake of believing God is promising to remove all of the obstacles we tend to bump into; He does not. However, He does promise to make our paths through these obstacles as straight as possible. He helps us not to get derailed and thrown off our tracks as we travel around these obstacles.

The value of this promise from God should be overwhelming. This is one promise that older people tend to see the value of more clearly than younger ones, as they have already stumbled over many more obstacles since they have been living for a longer period of time. The challenge is for them to find a way to share this understanding so that younger people will listen and see the relevance in their own lives. We must learn not to be condescending in our methods when we share with young people. A great way to accomplish this goal is by being honest with ourselves, and remembering how we used to be young in the same ways that they are now. We weren't easy to reach either when our elders tried to teach us what they had learned about life.

This passage from Proverbs also told us not to see ourselves as wise in our own eyes, which is a characteristic common to people of all ages. This is not a tendency found only in youthful people; it is present in all of us. To avoid this foolhardy behavior, we were told we must "fear the Lord, and shun evil."

The fact that we should learn to have a healthy fear of the Lord is a recurring theme throughout God's Word. We should have a fear of Him. When we consider His majesty and holiness; how can we not fear Him? One of the greatest misconceptions I believe people have about this lies in their failure to understand how a fear of God is healthy. It is like knowing not to touch a live electrical wire; you are better off because you have a fear of the exposed electrical power. You are less prone to suffering injury because of this fear; it is healthy for you.

We are also told this fear brings us rewards, and we can find such a promise in Psalm 111:10; "The fear of the Lord is the beginning of wisdom; all who follow his precepts have good understanding. To him belongs eternal praise." Here we are told that from this healthy type of fear we should have for God, we shall obtain wisdom. We need to see the patterns that emerge when we look at Scripture, such as the one present here. We know we should fear the Lord, and this will bring us to wisdom, and this wisdom will come from leaning on Him, and not on ourselves. One of our rewards from gaining this wisdom comes in our being able to maintain our stability as we travel through all of the twists and turns in this life.

If we open our hearts to this message contained there, we would see how it has been orchestrated by the greatest composer of all; and what a symphony He has created! When we read the Word and observe the beautiful way Scripture intertwines within itself, we will begin to marvel at the way God has shown us how to live our lives on this planet. Many different authors were inspired by God to write the books of the Bible, and they wrote them over a long period of time. But, they come together to form the most beautiful composition man has ever placed on paper. God's Word tells us why He inspired these men to write as they did in 2 Timothy 3:16–17; "All Scripture is God-breathed and is useful for teaching, rebuking, correcting and training in righteousness, so that the man of God may be thoroughly equipped for every good work."

Looking further into Scriptures speaking on this subject of not needing the crutch of Christianity, we turn to Proverbs 12:15; "The way of a fool seems wise to him, but a wise man listens to advice." Here we are reminded not to consider ourselves wise in our own eyes, because this will qualify us as the "fool" who is mentioned. Instead, be wise by listening to the good advice which comes from our Lord. If you do not, you are warned what will happen to you in Proverbs 14:12; "There is a way that seems right to a man, but in the end it leads to death." This is because the way that seems right to man is not God's way. It is like a famous man used to sing; "I did it my way!"

Believers do not choose Christianity because they need a crutch in order to stand. They choose Christianity because they know they can stand firmly when God is in control of their lives. We should not look at God's instructions as being a burden for us to bear, but rather as being there for our advantage. It is a privilege to be as we are told in Proverbs 20:24; "A man's steps are directed by the Lord. How then can anyone understand his own way?" We are truly blessed when we let God direct our steps; it allows us to travel on a straight path through life.

I pray these passages of Scripture have helped you to understand that Christianity is not a crutch for weak-minded people. The reality is quite the opposite, for Christianity is the only thing capable of making men truly strong. If we look at ourselves honestly, we will realize we aren't as strong and sure of ourselves as we try to lead others to believe. We read in Hosea 14:9; "Who is wise? He will realize these things. Who is discerning? He will understand them. The ways of the Lord are right; the righteous walk in them, but the rebellious stumble in them."

So when unbelievers use this "crutch" excuse, understand it is not the Christians who require a crutch! It is not the Christians who are weak-minded, because we have our God to teach us all we need to know. It is the non-believer who spends their entire lives searching for answers to the obstacles they stumble over in life. The believer has the answers to any questions life brings to them in God's Word. The non-believer keeps asking questions their whole life, and receives conflicting answers from as many sources as they go to for answers. They are really the ones looking for a crutch to lean on, which is why bookstores have shelves filled with "self-help" and "how-to" books. We need to pray for people to tire of moving from one crutch to another, and to find the only Rock on which anyone can ever stand firmly. For the Christian, that Rock is our Lord Jesus Christ; He is the Rock of our salvation!

It's Different *Now*, You Don't Understand

The next excuse is a saying many of us have heard and used ourselves; "Things are different now than when you grew up." My own children used this saying on my wife and myself throughout their entire upbringing. They still use it on occasions when I have a dispute with them over some tough set of circumstances. Our disagreements are usually over the solutions they come up with to handle those tough choices. This saying is just stating the obvious existence of the generation gap we discussed earlier. When we look at it closely, we find there is actually much more to it than just the gap.

If you think back on your teenage years and your early twenties, can you remember what it was like? Do you remember how things affected you, and your parents just didn't have a clue? I can remember that period in my life, and I remember how difficult of a time it was. It didn't matter how hard my parents tried to give me an answer to some crisis; I knew in my heart that they didn't understand. Remembering those beliefs I had as a teenager, made it easier for me to share with my own children when they got into similar struggles. Notice how I said it was easier to share with them; I did not say it was easier to guide them. This is because they were still teenagers, and they fell under the same belief system we were all under at that time.

After I was married and had a family of my own to raise, I talked about subjects like this with my parents. It was eye-opening to hear them tell me how they remembered going through the exact same thing with their parents before them. That is the point I am trying to get across here in these pages, and it is found in Ecclesiastes 1:9–10; "What has been will be again, what has been done will be done again; there is nothing new under the sun. Is there anything of which one can say, 'Look! This is something new'?"

The wisest person to ever live was a man named Solomon. He pointed out many profound truths for us in the book of Ecclesiastes. One of these truths is: no matter what we might want to believe, no situation we can find is unique and original only to us; everything has already been encountered. This truth applies to the generation gap, so there is nothing new about it. Examples which prove this are everywhere if we just look for them. One such example comes to mind from watching re-runs of old television programs. Do you remember the show called *Leave it to Beaver*? If you do, can you remember how the father, Ward Cleaver, reminisces quite often about how different it was for him growing up than it is for his own sons, Wally and Theodore (The Beaver)?

This popular show was originally aired in the 1950's, and the theme of the generation gap was there for all to see. The writers of this show simply recognized the existence of the generation gap, and used it for creating episodes that were humorous for us to watch. A more current example of this would be from the television show, *Everybody Loves Raymond*. In this popular series, Raymond and his family live across the street from his parents. Through comical situations, Raymond shows us how the generation gap created differences in his upbringing compared to that of his own children's.

Sitcom writers are quick to recognize the existence of the generation gap, and use it to create entertaining storylines for their shows. We as parents need to recognize this truth as well. When we do, we are more able to cope with our children's objections to our suggested solutions. To illustrate this fact, we can turn to some passages of Scripture dealing with this very situation, and one of them is found in the book of Job 12: 7–13:

> But ask the animals, and they will teach you, or the birds of the air, and they will tell you; or speak to the earth, and it will teach you, or let the fish of the sea inform you. Which of all these does not know that the hand of the Lord has done this? In his hand is the life of every creature and the breath of all mankind. Does not the ear test words as the tongue tastes food? Is not wisdom found among the aged? Does not long life bring understanding? To God belong wisdom and power; counsel and understanding are His.

This passage states clearly for us that all wisdom and power belong to God, and it also tells us the aged should have some of the wisdom and understanding which comes from walking with the Lord. Those who have been walking with God the longest should have gained the most wisdom and understanding from having spent time with Him. This is such an important point for us to understand. We need to walk with God in order to gain this wisdom and understanding. The longer we have been walking with Him in our lives, the wiser we should have become. This fact is mentioned in the book of Proverbs 20:29; "The glory of young men is their strength, gray hair the splendor of the old." Another similar passage is Proverbs 16:31; "Gray hair is a crown of splendor; it is attained by a righteous life."

Those of us, who have been walking long enough to have gray hair, should have also gained wisdom while trying to live righteously. Now let's look at what our Lord intended for us to do with this understanding He has promised to us. We are going to look at what God intended for us to do when working with the younger generation, and one place to turn is 1 Peter 5:1–5:

> To the elders among you, I appeal as a fellow elder, a witness of Christ's sufferings and one who also will share in the glory to be revealed: Be shepherds of God's flock that is under your care, serving as overseers—not because you must, but because you are willing, as God wants you to be; not greedy for money, but eager to serve; not lording it over those entrusted to you, but being examples to the flock. And when the Chief Shepherd appears, you will receive the crown of glory that will never fade away.
>
> Young men, in the same way be submissive to those who are older. All of you, clothe yourselves with humility toward one another, because, "God opposes the proud but gives grace to the humble."

This is how we should be shepherding our children, because they are part of the flock God has entrusted to our care. One of the best things we can do for our children is to be shining examples of what a person looks like when they are striving to be righteous before God. If we do this, they will want to follow in our ways and listen to our counseling when we offer it to them. Another shining passage on this topic is found in Titus 2:1–8:

> You must teach what is in accord with sound doctrine. Teach the older men to be temperate, worthy of respect, self-controlled, and sound in faith, in love and

> in endurance.
>
> Likewise, teach the older women to be reverent in the way they live, not to be slanderers or addicted to much wine, but to teach what is good. Then they can train the younger women to love their husbands and children, to be self-controlled and pure, to be busy at home, to be kind, and to be subject to their husbands, so that no one will malign the word of God.
>
> Similarly, encourage the young men to be self-controlled. In everything set them an example by doing what is good. In your teaching show integrity, seriousness and soundness of speech that cannot be condemned, so that those who oppose you may be ashamed because they have nothing bad to say about us.

What a couple of powerful passages of Scripture God gave to us in these verses! The older ones teaching the younger ones how to live, just by living the type of life which they are telling them they should be living! What a novel idea our Lord had in mind for us: to lead by example. We see how even two thousand years ago there was a generation gap between the older and younger generations. We also see how God supplied the answer for overcoming that gap, and His answer is the only one working for us today, just like it was then. We must strive to live the life of righteousness God has told us to live, and after they see our example, our young people will want to do the same.

For the young people God is talking about, there are passages to help them in their efforts to live this way. One such passage is found in Leviticus 19:32; "Rise in the presence of the aged, show respect for the elderly and revere your God. I am the Lord." Here we see where the custom of standing up for elders came from; it came from our Lord. God is telling us it is not only the elderly who we are showing respect towards when we do this; it is also for Him. Another passage can be found in Psalm 119:9–11; "How can a young man keep his way pure? By living according to your word. I seek you with all my heart; do not let me stray from your commands. I have hidden your word in my heart that I might not sin against you."

Young people, pay attention to the commands God has given to you. And for you who are not so young, put those commands to use in your life so the young can see them in practice. This is the command given to those who have lived long enough to have gray in our hair, and we need to obey it. Another common thought I had as a young adult, and that many young adults still have today, is the feeling that the older generation was looking down on me because of my youth. I felt it when I was younger, and I believe many of you are feeling the same way today.

If at times you do feel like the older generation is looking down on you, I urge you to read from the book of 1 Timothy 4:12–13; "Don't let anyone look down on you because you are young, but set an example for the believers in speech, in life, in love, in faith and in purity. Until I come, devote yourself to the public reading of Scripture, to preaching and to teaching."

The reason the young are told to do this is obvious; no one will be able to look down on you for your being young when you are living the life the aged are supposed to be living. What a wonderful thought, to think of the younger generation setting the example for the older generation by living the life that all true believers are supposed to be living. If you do this, you will overcome the generation gap. God has promised that to you.

I'm Too Cool

This next excuse was shared by a group of young people, but we shall see how it can easily be responsible for the failings of any age group. The expression used was, "I'm too cool to be a Christian." This statement implies Christians are not hip to this world; it is a correct statement. We are not meant to be cool in the sense of being "special" or "idolized." We are just trying to live our lives in the way God has instructed us. When we look at this condition of being "too cool" for God, we need to see through it to its root thought: I am too proud to be a Christian.

This nature of pride has been around since sin entered the world, and it is in full force today. We can all fall victim to this nature, and be found guilty of pride in ourselves, in our accomplishments, in our possessions, and countless other areas. We can get puffed up about ourselves. We have already seen how the young can be proud of their youthful strength, but there's so much more involved when looking at this subject of pride. To look more deeply into this subject, we can turn to Jeremiah 9:23–24:

> This is what the Lord says: "Let not the wise man boast of his wisdom or the strong man boast of his strength or the rich man boast of his riches, but let him who boasts boast about this: that he understands and knows me, that I am the Lord, who exercises kindness, justice and righteousness on earth, for in these I delight," declares the Lord.

We are told in Jeremiah not to feel so proud of ourselves that we are lead to the point of boasting about things such as our strength, riches, or knowledge. This is the sin of pride, and we must strive to overcome its clutches on our hearts. This spirit takes hold of us and leads us to boasting about ourselves and our accomplishments. There are many warnings in Scripture for us about this downfall, which should tell us it is very common and very dangerous for us. Proverbs 29:23 says, "A man's pride brings him low, but a man of lowly spirit gains honor."

This verse points out that it is because of a man's pride in himself, he will be brought down. At the same time, it tells us a man who is lowly in spirit will gain honor. This honor will come from God, and is not something we are trying to receive from other men. Another passage found in Jesus Christ's Sermon on the Mount touches on this subject as well. Matthew 5:3 reads, "Blessed are the poor in spirit, for theirs is the kingdom of heaven." Our Lord says those of us who are not proud of spirit will be truly happy, and will inherit the kingdom of heaven.

This spirit of pride is mentioned throughout God's Word. I am listing a few of the references here so you can see the effort God put into warning us about this existence of pride. One such passage can be found in the book of Proverbs 21:4; "Haughty eyes and a proud heart, the lamp of the wicked, are sin!" This Scripture tells us the pride in the hearts and the eyes of people serves as their lamp; it is what shines for them in their walk. This lamp they use as their light is called sin, and God issued a stern warning for all who are guilty of this proud nature.

For further warning, we can look at Proverbs 16:5 and 16:18; "The Lord detests all the proud of heart. Be sure of this: They will not go unpunished;" and this, "Pride goes before destruction, a haughty spirit before a fall." Warnings, warnings, and more warnings for those guilty of pride; please, heed these warnings! Throw off this spirit of pride which causes us to look at ourselves instead of looking towards God! It is not cool to be proud and boast about yourself; if you want to be cool, boast about God!

Another warning on this topic is found in the book of Daniel 4:37b; "Praise, exalt, and glorify the King of heaven, because everything he does is right and all his ways are just. And those who walk in pride he is able to humble." God is the one we are to exalt and glorify, He alone is worthy of praise and adoration. None of us are, and that is why none of us should boast about ourselves. A couple more passages reinforcing this concept are 1 Corinthians 1:31; "Therefore, as it is written: Let him who boasts boast in the Lord." Also, 2 Corinthians 10:17–18; "Let him who boasts boast in the Lord. For it is not the one who commends himself who is approved, but the one whom the Lord commends."

I urge you to pay close attention to the latter of these. In his writing these passages, Paul has warned those of us who are proud, and think of ourselves as being "too cool." They will not be the ones who are commended by our Lord. Remember what our Lord said in the Sermon on the Mount; "Blessed are the poor in spirit." Those who do not hold themselves up high are the ones who will be blessed. If you think of yourself as being "too cool" to allow even a consideration of Christianity in your life, reflect on these passages of Scripture. Ask God to speak to your heart, and He will show you the error of your prideful nature. Then you will be able to put away your prideful behavior, which will keep you from enjoying the blessings of God.

Earlier, we read how the apostle Paul thought he had much to boast about concerning his own nature, but Jesus showed him his error. He is trying to show all of us this same thing, if we will just look at ourselves in a mirror reflecting our true nature. After we see ourselves for what we really are, we can come to the place of being "poor in spirit." When you get there, you will agree with what Paul says in one of my favorite passages of Scripture, found in the book of Galatians 6:14; "May I never boast except in the cross of our Lord Jesus Christ, through which the world has been crucified to me, and I unto the world." Amen.

If you are one of the many people who believe they don't need God because they are tough enough to take it, and strong enough to stand on their own, you are very mistaken. There is nobody out there who is so "cool" that God will accept them as they are. Nobody is as tough as they try to be. Our Lord Jesus is the only one who has ever measured up to the standards God set forth for us all; He is the only one who ever will! It is only when we let Him cover our sins through His sacrifice on the Cross that we are found acceptable before God.

We must remember God's standard includes living a life without sin, and we read in Romans 3:23; "For all have sinned and fall short of the glory of God." Maybe you can convince yourself God didn't mean "all" as in "everybody" when He gave us this verse; but He did. There is nobody who has ever qualified for God's righteousness, except for Jesus Christ Himself. There will never be anyone else who qualifies in the future. That is what this verse means, and there is no loophole to be found in God's statement. Jesus is the only way by which we can achieve righteousness.

When you contemplate your position in life, do not let yourself be fooled by the world into believing your time is somehow different than anyone else's before you; it is not. Do not make the mistake of thinking Christians are somehow nothing but a bunch of wimps who need a crutch to stand on; we are not. When it comes time to stand up during the worst of times life has to offer us, Christians are the ones who have the Rock to lean on to ride out any storm they may encounter. It is the believer who can take it; not the unbeliever. God is not looking for people who want to do it their own way; He is looking for people who will strive to do it His way.

In the end, you will not be standing at all if you go through this life on your own; instead, you will be kneeling in shame before God on His throne. You will not find yourself thinking you are "too cool" when you find yourself there, begging for mercy from God. You will know what it means in Hebrews 10:31; "It is a dreadful thing to fall into the hands of the living God." The warning is plain to see in this verse that all who think they don't need God are very wrong. We all need God whether we admit it or not; it is a fact of life. God designed us with this in mind, but He gave us the option of deciding for ourselves whether or not to accept His love for us. We do not have to. We can go throughout our lives in defiance of His will. If you are going to do this, just do not fool yourself into believing you will not pay in the end, because you will.

If you want to be a real "cool" man or woman, then stand up with the help of God. Proclaim to others the wonder of His mercy. Yell from the mountaintops that He is Lord over all, and tell people just like Solomon did in Ecclesiastes 1:9; "What has been will be again, what has been done will be done again; there is nothing new under the sun." People try to deny this fact, but it remains the truth; things are no different today than they were at any other time. What has been will be again, just as Solomon said.

If you really want to boast of something, boast of the love God has shown for us. Accept the gift of eternal life that Jesus Christ offered at the Cross, and become a servant of the living God. You will find out you are standing more firmly than you ever had before! You will find out what it really means to be strong, and in the strength God gives to you, you can help lead others to the same understanding. We all need someone to help lead us there so we don't fall into the hands of the living God; instead, we will be picked up by them!

Chapter Seven

It's Too Early/Too Late for Me

In this chapter, we will be looking at the excuse of it being the wrong time in life for someone to consider Christianity. As the title suggests, we will be looking at both ends of our human time-line—the beginning and the end. This is another excuse offered by people I have talked with, and we will look at some of their thoughts. I am also going to share some of my own thoughts on these subjects, based on dealing with them as part of my own "excuse" background.

I'm Still Young

There are two totally different trains of thought which I have found grouped under the "too early" heading. First let's look at the concept of whether or not someone is too young to become a Christian. Does the Bible teach us that there is a certain age at which someone is capable of receiving salvation?

No, because there is not a numerical value given in Scripture defining the age at which a child becomes accountable for their actions. Each individual will become accountable at different ages, because we all mature at different levels and speeds. In order to ask for salvation, we must first be able to recognize our need for it. Since all children mature at different rates, there cannot be a standard age which encompasses all under a single umbrella. In order to determine whether an individual child is at an age when they are ready to understand their own behavior, turn to the book of Proverbs 20:11; "Even a child is known by his actions, by whether his conduct is pure and right."

An important concept from this verse is the concept of being known by our actions. The word *action* refers to acts of the will being done in a deliberate, thought out, and preconceived manner. It is in reference to acts which children perform through their own willful desires. We are told that after children (not babies) begin performing willful actions of their own, we should be able to look at whether their conduct is pure and right. We are told that once children reach this stage of accountability, they become much like adults in knowing right from wrong and choosing which path to follow.

Acts 26:20b says, "I preached that they should repent and turn to God and prove their repentance by their deeds." This is one of the standards for living a Christian life as God set forth for us, and it should be applied to children as well as adults. The key lies in whether or not a child is at the age of committing willful actions. If they are still too immature to understand their actions, they are also still too immature to understand their need for salvation.

This does not mean we should stand by and wait for our children to become mature young people before we teach them about Christianity; that is not the case at all. Instead, we are to do as told in Proverbs 22:6; "Train a child in the way he should go, and when he is old he will not turn from it." These instructions for parents are very clear and precise: start training your children when they are young, so they will be prepared to live as they ought to when they are older. This does not mean we can make them into Christians, because they will have to make that choice once they are mature enough to understand their need for salvation. It means we should teach them about God by reading His Word to them as much as possible. This training will be the beginning of their understanding of God, and that is what we are told to teach them.

Another good passage looking at the maturing of children is found in 1 Corinthians 13:11; "When I was a child, I talked like a child, I thought like a child, I reasoned like a child. When I became a man, I put childish ways behind me." The Apostle Paul is telling us that adults are not to behave like little children. This is because little children are not able to reason over their actions. The ability to reason over our actions is what is called the age of accountability. Once a child reaches this maturity level, they become capable of understanding their need for salvation. Each child will reach this maturity at different ages, which is why we cannot generalize any certain age at which a child can be saved.

Paul gives us another example of leaving childish ways behind in 1 Corinthians 14:20; "Brothers, stop thinking like children. In regard to evil be infants, but in your thinking be adults." Our behavior towards evil should be just like that of young children; they do not desire to do evil with bad intentions. This is an example of adults needing to be childlike in attitude towards evil, but we are clearly told to reason as adults. In looking at these last two passages, we see the command telling us we must humble ourselves like little children. We must trust completely in God just as children trust completely in their parents. We also see that we are to stop behaving as little children once we mature, and start thinking like adults.

All of us as parents must obey the instructions we looked at in the book of Proverbs, and train our children in the way they should grow. We need to teach them the Lord's commandments so they will know right from wrong, and so they will understand there are consequences for not obeying them. This will serve as the cornerstone for them in the future after they become adults, which is why it is so important we start teaching them at a very young age. Nobody knows the level of their child's maturity better than the child's father and mother, and they should know when their child has reached the age of accountability. As we saw in the book of Proverbs, "The child will be known by their actions." Parents are the best judges of whether those actions are willful or not.

A thought which I have heard from others is that we are "wasting our time" when we share with young children God's plan for their lives. This mistaken view comes from believing children are "too young" to understand, so why share with them? It is true young children may not be able to offer a solid explanation of what it means to be a Christian, but what of it? If your children are only able to recite Christian rhymes, and short Bible verses and stories, it is a beginning. The ability to do these things is the first sign of God's presence in your children; praise God for them! Do not make the mistake of waiting to start teaching your children about God and His kingdom until you think they are "old enough to get it." At what age do you think the world begins to exert its influence on your children? With that thought in mind, I pray we all understand there is no such thing as being "too early" in sharing with our children about God; start as soon as they have ears to hear, and eyes to see!

Another excuse dealing with being "too young for Christianity" comes from people who say it is just "too early" in life to become a Christian. Let's look at this excuse which is offered by individuals who say they are going to wait until they are "older" before they consider choosing Christianity for their lives. This is an excuse I am very familiar with myself, because I used to think the same way when I was a young man.

One of the most obvious mistakes in this way of thinking is the simple fact that we can never know exactly how long we have to live on this earth in the first place. Cemeteries are full of the remains of dead people, who left this world long before they had planned. It is a fact of life; death comes for us all. None of us have a guarantee saying we will reach whatever age we consider to be old, before we will pass away. We are not even guaranteed the next day. An example of this fact can be found in the book of Luke 12:16–20:

> And He told them this parable: "The ground of a certain rich man produced a good crop. He thought to himself, 'What shall I do? I have no place to store my crops.'
>
> Then he said, 'This is what I'll do. I will tear down my barns and build bigger ones, and there I will store all my grain and my goods.' And I'll say to myself, 'You have plenty of good things laid up for many years. Take life easy; eat, drink, and be merry.'

> But God said to him, 'You fool! This very night your life will be demanded from you. Then who will get what you have prepared for yourself?'"

We can see from this parable, how God warned us not to get so wrapped up in ourselves, that we forget about our own mortality. We are also told how we should not spend too much effort and energy on accumulating possessions for ourselves here on this earth. In order to expose the futility of planning on waiting to consider Christianity at a later time in one's life, the meaning could not be clearer: you may not get to later. Therefore, do not put off until tomorrow what you need to do now; in case tomorrow never arrives for you.

This is why we are to witness with such urgency to those with whom we come into contact. We do not know how long they will have to decide about their eternal existence before they actually leave this life and move on to wherever they will spend the rest of eternity. The difficulty comes from the fact that youth believe in their strength, and cannot see their own mortality as a truth of reality yet. This is one of the conditions I remember well from when I was a young man. However, as life often does, I was given a wake-up call at an early age; I lost a younger brother at the age of twenty to a type of cancerous lymphoma. I thank God for the fact that my brother was a born-again believer, and I look forward to the day when we shall see each other again in Heaven! The circumstances surrounding my brother's illness served notice for all of us who were close to him, and taught us plainly how our mortality was something we had better not ignore. Ever since that time, I have understood how fragile my own existence truly is, and this understanding has served me well.

Another passage of Scripture warning us against waiting

to take Christianity seriously can be found in Luke 12:40; "You also must be ready, because the Son of Man will come at an hour when you do not expect Him." We are to be prepared to greet our Lord when He returns; at whatever time it happens. We are not told when He will return, only that He will. This is another reason why you should never wait until later to consider your salvation. Nobody knows if Jesus will wait to return until you are older, any more than you know if you will make it to old age. The real question is whether or not it is worth the gamble you are taking when thinking in this manner; I wholeheartedly say to you that it is not!

When I think back to my own youth, I remember the reasons prompting me to think about waiting until I had reached old age before I would take Christ seriously. As we have already learned from looking at God's teaching in the book of Ecclesiastes 1:9b; "There is nothing new under the sun." Using this verse as my guide, I believe I can still relate to what may be motivating you now if you are guilty of this excuse; just as I was in my youth. I remember the things I used to think were so important to me, and it was these things I wanted to do and have which misled me when I was young.

I remember wanting to "sow my wild oats," as the world says. I wanted to run with the pack, and with the opposite sex. I wanted to be free and do whatever I felt like. I didn't want anyone or anything to tell me I couldn't do whatever I wanted, or that it was wrong if I did. I didn't want to submit to anyone's rules or regulations; especially God's. I believed completely in God's existence, but there was no way I would submit to His will, yet. That was the real motivation behind my wanting to wait. I had enough Bible knowledge in me to know I would have to quit doing a lot of the things I liked to do if I were a Christian. I was living under the influence of my flesh, and I wasn't ready to leave my lifestyle of sin. I knew I wanted to be saved, but thought I could play it my way first, and just wait until I had done all of those things I believed would bring me so much pleasure.

This was the way I thought I could manipulate my own salvation, and perhaps it is the way you think, also. If it is, then turn with me to Proverbs 14:12; "There is a way that seems right to a man, but in the end it leads to death." What a strong warning against this mistaken belief in our own ability to "time" our salvation out until we have lived a life of sin long enough to satisfy our flesh. This belief can lead us to our eternal death! We are told our sin will lead us to this very kind of death in Romans 6:23; "For the wages of sin is death, but the gift of God is eternal life in Christ Jesus our Lord."

We need to realize this death the Apostle Paul warns us about in the book of Romans is not only the physical one which we all will go through here on earth. It is also the spiritual one we will suffer if we leave this life without having received Christ's gift offered on the Cross. I cannot warn you strongly enough against this condition of "timing out" our Christianity. You do not know the timetable for your life, so you cannot afford to wait one minute longer! I remember the times from my youth when I listened to pastors preaching and urging those listening to make a commitment to God. I remember how I shrugged them off. I was in the same place you may be in right now, and even though it was almost thirty years ago now, I can vividly remember dismissing the pleas of those who were trying to lead me to Christ.

I remember very well how I shrugged them off, but I also remember the way I lay awake at night and wondered if I was making some great mistake in doing so. Although I tried to convince myself I would just wait until later, there was always this gnawing feeling which told me I had better not. As I said earlier, the experience of my brother's passing was enough to show me the error in my way of thinking. My salvation has served as proof for me of the truth in Romans 8:28; "And we know that in all things God works for the good of those who love Him, who have been called according to His purpose." Even in something as tragic as the passing of my brother, God worked good out of it in my life! My parents struggle with my brother's death to this day, but they have had peace from knowing their other son's salvation came about largely because of his untimely passing.

As one who overcame this excuse, I want you to know that I can say with the utmost sincerity that none of those things I thought were so important have turned out to be as important as I thought. The thrills I used to crave from the sinful lifestyle do not compare in any way with the ones I have felt since I became a born-again believer! It can be so difficult to help an unbeliever understand the euphoria which comes from being saved, but it is a challenge all believers must try to overcome. If you have not succeeded in accomplishing this task in your life as yet, I am praying for God to send someone into your life who will help you to finish the job which I am trying to help you start.

I pray that God touches you in a way you may never have felt before in your heart; and for this stirring to cause you to lie awake at night wondering about your hesitance for Christ. Do not hesitate. Instead, ask God to touch your heart and soften it for you. Open your eyes and read His Word. Listen to the messengers God places in front of you to share His Word. You must find a way to get yourself to the point where you can do as it says in Romans 10:9–10; "That if you confess with your mouth, 'Jesus is Lord,' and believe in your heart that God raised Him from the dead, you will be saved. For it is with your heart that you believe and are justified, and it is with your mouth that you confess and are saved."

This is the position you must put yourself into, and to put off making that decision for any reason is utter foolishness! Do not be found guilty of having waited too long. If you do, you will spend your eternity separated from the love of God! That is the definition of hell, and no one in their right mind should risk the possibility of spending their eternity there! What a perilous position you find yourself in when you procrastinate about your salvation. I know it seems like you will be around for a very long time, but will you really? Do you have inside information on your checkout date? If you did, I suppose you could feel like you are on top of everything, and you would think it will all work out in the long run. I know I didn't have that kind of information about my life span when I was a young man, and I don't believe any of you do either.

That fact alone should be enough to make you lie awake in bed, and ponder your foolishness. Snap out of it! Don't walk; run to Jesus! He is the only one who can save you, just as it says in the book of John 14:6; "Jesus answered, I am the way and the truth and the life. No one comes to the Father except through me." Jesus Christ is the only one who can save your soul from eternal punishment. There is none other, and there is no other way. I pray you have been pointed in the right direction, and for God to help you listen to those who plead for your souls more than I listened to the pleas of others in my youth. Whatever you may decide, just do it soon.

Remember, if you choose not to receive God's gift of eternal life, you have still made a decision. If you can at least admit to the truth in that, then you will not find yourself trying to tell God how you were waiting until later when you are called to stand before Him to give an account for yourself. I hope that thought does what needs to be done in your heart. I know it kept me awake at night when I was young, and living under this condition. If we admit the truth, we will realize how foolish of a position it is to be in. All we have to do is take the leap of faith, and do it now; not later.

I'm Too Old Now

Let's move on and look at some excuses used in dismissing one's salvation based on the opinion it is too late. The first example comes from the concept of it being too late, because there would not be enough time to make it worthwhile to try. Before tackling this thought, I want to remind you of the obvious fact we just looked at: we do not even know how much time there is for us in the first place. How can we determine it is too late, when we don't know how late in life it really is? It is never too late until we are no longer living; then it is too late.

I can understand the reasoning behind thinking if we have waited until very late in our lives here on earth, it might not be worth the effort to change since we have already wasted so much of the time we were given. But this is not the way God sees it. He says we are worth saving no matter what our condition is, and that includes whether we are elderly, or just think of ourselves as elderly. God does not say there is an age we will reach when we become "not worth the effort." Christ died for all of us, with no regard of our ages.

A great illustration of this fact can be found in the book of Matthew 20:1–15:

For the kingdom of Heaven is like a landowner who went out early in the morning to hire men to work in his vineyard. He agreed to pay them a denarius for the day and sent them into his vineyard.

About the third hour he went out and saw others standing in the marketplace doing nothing. He told them, "You also go and work in my vineyard, and I will pay you whatever is right," so they went.

He went out again about the sixth hour and the ninth hour and did the same thing. About the eleventh hour he went out and found still others standing around. He asked them, "Why have you been standing here all day long doing nothing?"

"Because no one hired us," they answered.

He said to them, "You also go and work in my vineyard."

When evening came, the owner of the vineyard said to his foreman, "Call the workers and pay them their wages, beginning with the last ones hired and going to the first."

The workers who were hired about the eleventh hour came and each received a denarius. So when those came who were hired first, they expected to receive more. But each one of them also received a denarius. When they received it, they began to grumble against the landowner, "These men who were hired last worked

> only one hour," they said, "and you have made them equal to us who have borne the burden of the work and the heat of the day."
>
> But he answered one of them, "Friend, I am not being unfair to you. Didn't you agree to work for a denarius? Take your pay and go. I want to give the man who was hired last the same as I gave you. Don't I have the right to do what I want with my own money? Or are you envious because I am generous?"

In this parable, Jesus was letting us know that the workers who join Him near the ends of their lives, will receive the same reward as those who start their service early in life. The final reward is eternal life with Him in Heaven. It makes no difference at what time in our lives we receive this gift He suffered and died for; the reward remains the same. We can see man's logic in the complaints of those who began their service much earlier in life, but we must accept the generosity of God being able to bestow His gift on whomever He wants and whenever He wants. Who are we to question God's generosity? We should rejoice with equal enthusiasm for anyone who receives Christ as Savior, and their age at the time is irrelevant.

God's Word does not say when we reach any certain age we move past the possibility of salvation just because we will not have enough time to be fruitful in Christ's service. This parable completely destroys that position! We are clearly shown there is no age when we become undesirable to God. This does not mean, as we have looked at earlier, that we can plan on receiving our salvation on our death bed. I have heard it preached in this way, "I do not believe that death bed conversions are impossible; but I do believe they are highly improbable." That is the point of what we looked at earlier when dealing with trying to "time out" our salvation.

Another example we can use against this excuse of being "too late" is found in the book of Luke 23: 39–43:

> One of the criminals who hung there hurled insults at Him; "Aren't you the Christ? Save yourself and us!" But the other criminal rebuked him, "Don't you fear God," he said, "since you are under the same sentence? We are punished justly, for we are getting what our deeds deserve. But this man has done nothing wrong." Then he said, "Jesus, remember me when you come into your kingdom." Jesus answered him, "I tell you the truth, today you will be with me in paradise."

Luke has given us an excellent example to look at here, and we should pay close attention to the conversation which took place between Jesus and this thief. It was in the closing moments of this thief's life when he asked Jesus to remember him when He went to Heaven. This man told Jesus with all of his heart, that he wanted Christ to remember him. He wanted Jesus to remember him, and to know he was sorry for the evil way he had lived his life. He wanted Jesus to remember him, and to forgive him. Jesus knew his repentance was real. Jesus told him they would be in paradise together, and He forgave him. Jesus wanted him to know he had been forgiven, and told him what his reward would be.

We are not told the age of this thief, but we know he died shortly after he was forgiven by Christ. He certainly didn't have time to do many good works after his conversion, or to change the way he was living on this earth. But Jesus didn't tell him it was too late for him. He didn't say you are past the point of usefulness in my kingdom. He simply eased his suffering by letting him know how great the reward which now awaited him in heaven was. This thief was not going to have time to gain many crowns through serving the Lord; but he was still going to join Him in paradise!

This fact is one which deserves our close attention, which is why Luke wrote it down for us. We are shown how we can be saved even at the very last hour of our life; as long as our repentance is real and we sincerely desire forgiveness. So we should never believe it is too late for any of us as long as we have breath in us.

This thief is in heaven waiting for us to get there. Even though he didn't get to serve the Lord and earn rewards in Heaven, it is still something so magnificent, the angels rejoiced over his salvation! Let this thought put to rest any reasoning trying to tell you that anybody is beyond being worthwhile for salvation. It is never too late to be saved while we are still breathing, and it will always be the best thing to ever happen to you, no matter when in life it takes place!

Now for a slightly different angle on this "too late" excuse, let's look at the individual who says they have tried to change before; but it didn't work. This excuse has been used in a similar fashion to the previous one, only with a slightly different twist. It reminds me of a popular expression; "you can't teach an old dog new tricks." When I hear someone share this feeling, I turn it around on them and use another popular expression in return; "if at first you don't succeed, try, try again."

When someone really understands what is at stake in this process of salvation, they will never cease trying to receive it. This excuse comes from people who have only partially seen the truth of God's gift. If they can be helped to see clearly what is available, they will never stop striving for it. So in response to those who believe they have already made a sincere effort to attain their forgiveness, I urge you to keep on trying. This process should be much like the one smokers use when trying to quit: never quit quitting. Seeking one's forgiveness is very similar in the way we should be continually striving for God's forgiveness, even after we know we have already received it. Once you know you have received it, you should continually thank Him for it.

The most important thing to remember is to never stop trying. The motivation needed to keep trying should be the simple understanding that if we fail, we will spend eternity in total separation from God; which is called Hell. This fact alone should be all the motivation one needs to pursue their salvation through whatever obstacles this world can throw against us.

What can it possibly mean if we feel we have tried before, and it didn't work? I have found the most common instance for creating this feeling is when someone says they have tried God's way, but it just didn't work for them. Much of the time, this comes from the fact they tried to believe in their minds, but not first with their hearts. This seems to be the common denominator when looking at people using this excuse. When they made what they call their attempt at living a Christian life, they tried to do it under their own power. They made a decision in their minds to change the way they live. The mistake comes when they believe they can do so through only their own efforts. We have looked at many passages showing us this will never work for us; we cannot do it on our own.

My advice to those of you who feel as if you have already made an honest effort at living a Christian life, but failed in the trying, is that you should try again after first admitting you need a change to take place in your heart. If you do not have a change taking place in your heart, your confession with your mouth will be irrelevant. This is the reason why so many of us feel we have failed in previous attempts at Christian living.

If you can see this in yourself, then you must try again. You should never give up on yourself. God doesn't give up on us. This might seem like a very simple response to this excuse; but it is the best one. If you truly feel you have tried and failed, it's no excuse to stop trying. You must renew your efforts in asking God to soften your heart, so you can see your need for forgiveness and become truly repentant for your sins. If you do this, Jesus promises you will be forgiven. You will no longer say you have failed. You will have succeeded in attaining the highest prize available to man; you will be saved!

So looking at this excuse of thinking it is too late to make a decision for Christ, I hope you have come to the understanding that death is the only thing which can make it too late. Death is the only thing which can stop us from changing our decision. Do not be deceived by thoughts like, "you have been this way too long to change now;" it is only the enemy's attempt at causing you to give up on yourself. Do not listen to him. It does not matter if you will only have a short time to serve our Lord. It does not matter if you will have no time to serve at all—you are still worth the effort.

So the next time you find yourself thinking it is too late for you, please remember the examples of the thief on the cross and the workers in the vineyard. God promises His gift of salvation to all who believe in His Son, with no minimum time requirements. Maybe you will be someone who is saved just like the thief on the cross—during your final moments on this earth. Maybe you will be like one of the last of the workers in the vineyard, and you will only have a short time to serve the Lord. In either case, time is not what's important. What's important is for you to realize you are worth as much to God as any other human being who has ever lived. This alone should be enough to help you to see you are worth the effort, no matter what your age or how many times you have tried and failed before. Never stop trying until you know you are saved, because no matter what you have thought before, God's Word says you are worth the effort!

Chapter Eight

I'm Busy Trying Something Else

This chapter has been more difficult to put into words than the previous ones. The following excuses were offered more as explanations of behaviors rather than as a dismissal of Christianity. These people feel they have found something other than Jesus Christ to fill the void in their lives. They believe they have found a purpose for their lives, and therefore they have no need of Christianity.

Most of these behaviors are going to be examples of the many ways we as humans try to fill the space in our hearts which God has used to place our need for His presence. Many call this place the "God-shaped hole" in our hearts. The mistaken attempts by people to fill this hole with something other than God are what we will be looking at in this chapter. Many of these fillers people use are not religions in their own right, but they do fulfill many of the qualities found in religious organizations. Although they may be disguised as many different things, they are nothing more than alternatives to Christianity.

To start this look into "religious substitutes" for Christianity, let's turn to the definition of religion as offered in Webster's. It is described as "a cause, principle, or system of beliefs held to with ardor and faith." Webster's does not require some type of deity to be included in order to qualify as being a system of religious activity. This same definition is used to explain why someone who participates in some activity on a regular basis is said to be performing that activity "religiously." An example would be the way someone participates in an exercise program, how they watch a particular television program, or anything else they do with this sense of "must do it" being involved in the activity.

I'm a Supporter of Secularism

A good example to illustrate this point is secularism. Webster's defines this as "a system that ranges from indifference to rejection or exclusion of religion or any religious considerations." Our society is very familiar with this concept of secularism. It permeates every inch of our world, and is surrounded by the catch phrase of being "politically correct," which we looked at earlier. Secularism is a state of being, which qualifies under the definition of religion as stated in Webster's. The people who are pushing this position are definitely ardent and faithful in their support of this cause and its system of beliefs. For them, it can very well be their religion.

Many of those who are so actively involved in forcing the so-called separation of church and state in our country claim they are doing so because our founding fathers wanted to keep any reference to God out of our government. They are willing to ignore, or more accurately, distort the historical record showing quite the opposite to be true. One of the characteristics of this movement which stands out like a beacon is how if you want to believe a certain position, you will. It will not matter whether or not someone can offer conclusive proof contrary to their position; they deem that proof to be irrelevant, inconclusive, or misinterpreted. The overwhelming desire to achieve a certain set of circumstances will override all other considerations.

The proponents of this secularist society have pushed this agenda forward with all the zeal they can muster. This movement has been sweeping across our country like a wildfire raging out of control. Those behind it have all the traits attached to religious zealots, and they serve their chosen religion with every ounce of their being. They speak about how important it is to keep all of our public policies and governmental institutions pure—free from religious references of any kind. They believe these public arenas can be pure on their own, and they are the ones keeping them so. They do not recognize it is God who is the one who makes all things pure, not man.

Secularism is nothing more than an extension of humanistic belief in man's own value being transferred from man directly to man's institutions and societies. It is the natural step following the belief in man as the highest form of life in the universe, and the belief in man having the answer to all of his problems. These individuals are using secularism as an alternative to Christianity, because they are not really just pushing a system keeping God out of the public lifestyle; they are pushing a system which is an alternative to a Godly lifestyle. The humanistic view has transposed itself into the secularist's view of society, and is replacing the importance of God in public life with the absence of it.

One of the saddest things about this whole agenda is that these individuals do not see how they are trying to replace God with this grand notion they call secularism. They do not seem to realize they are dismissing the value of the Creator of the Universe, and in effect are denying His very existence. Many of them claim to believe in God, but their actions are those of an atheist. You can't believe in God as the ultimate authority in the universe, but cut Him out of the process of governing our society.

People on news programs state they are not trying to "get rid" of God. They say they are not claiming He doesn't exist; yet their actions show they do not recognize Him as God. The saddest individuals of all are the ones who claim to believe in God, but say He should be kept out of our public arenas. This is an oxymoron of the worst kind! If you truly know God, then you will also know He is the only hope of good things happening in any and all of our public arenas!

If you find yourself believing this misguided concept, please reconsider whether or not you have truly accepted the reality of God's existence. Once you have seen the truth of God's existence, you could never try to limit His influence over anything! To follow this secularist movement is to deny the sovereignty of God, because no one can try to place any limitations upon Him if they really understand who He is. To live in a secular way with great zeal is merely an attempt to fill our need for God with the importance of man and his society. Do not deceive yourself with false notions of being a Christian, if you still believe it is right to place limitations on what God should be allowed to do and where He should be allowed to go. I know this will stand in the faces of those who profess Christ as Savior, but follow this humanist type of belief system; but I must ask you a question, "What is man that he should dictate to God?"

Man is so full of himself, and he sees himself as the ultimate authority in this universe. This vision is what forms the basis for humanism and secularism; they are replacement religions for Christianity. Do not deceive yourselves into believing you can be both a zealous Christian and humanist/ secularist, because you can't. The Christian sees the futile nature of man, and this understanding is incompatible with a system which exalts man and his societal institutions. To lift man up, is to go against the foundational Biblical doctrines of "dying to self" and taking up one's Cross and following Christ.

I Have a Therapist

Another method people use to try and satisfy the void in their life we call our God-shaped hole, is to visit with psychologists and psychiatrists. This is something which can even be considered to be in vogue. To have your own therapist can be rated as a status symbol of prestige. Professionals in these fields can be beneficial when we seek Christian-oriented specialists to help whenever a need for them arises.

One potential problem area with these fields of medicine is the way they choose to define and describe the problems people bring to them for treatment. A good example would be how just the other night while watching a news brief on television, I saw a feature on the gambling problem which has surfaced in college students. There was a professor being interviewed, who has performed a study paid for by a governmental grant. He described the devastation being wreaked upon these students and their families who support them. An example was given of one student who robbed a bank to cover the losses he suffered through his gambling habit, along with other situations which were more common among those students involved with gambling. It was pointed out how the Internet has made access to these gambling facilities so easy to achieve, and this was offered as one of the number one causes for the ill-effects these students were suffering.

The news story then took a turn for the worse, as they went to visit a psychologist who had specialized in this area. He proceeded to explain how this phenomenon was nothing more than a new "health hazard" our children are facing. He explained how this addiction to gambling was nothing more than just an illness which these students were suffering from. It is this type of attitude which I hold out as being inferior when comparing secular psychologists/psychiatrists with Christian-oriented ones. If you have a need for a professional in either of these fields, please choose one who follows Biblical principles.

There are a number of so-called illnesses and addictions which cause people to seek help from professionals in overcoming, but the question must be asked; are these doctors really looking at the root of their problem? There seems to be a tendency to excuse many of these types of "illnesses" as simply being health problems, which can be cured through the use of medications and therapy sessions.

Using drugs as a method to treat the symptoms these problems produce does not help the individual discover what is leading to this behavior in the first place. It is another attempt by man to excuse his sinful nature, through labeling much of the sinful activities which he participates in as merely being addictions and illnesses. If you suffer from one of these types of "illnesses," you need to look inside yourself to discover why you are really involved in whatever "addiction" happens to be your personal downfall.

People talk about their need to experience the "high" coming from gambling, alcohol, prescription and non-prescription drugs, sex, pornography, and many other activities. They are only described as addictions when they are involved in amounts considered to be beyond reasonable. These individuals need to look inside themselves, and honestly decide why they are involved in these activities at all. Why are they looking to provide themselves with this short-term pleasure? What is it they are trying to satisfy inside themselves? Are they searching for that long-term joy which only comes from a relationship with God? Are they substituting these other activities for the one thing which could truly satisfy them?

Twenty-first century man has found new avenues to make his pursuits easier, such as the internet, but although the avenue may be new, the end reached is the same as ever; sinful behavior. This is where people can be misled by secular reasoning, and by professionals who use secular wisdom. These types of activities are definitely a problem for those involved, but they are not simply stricken with an illness as much as they are just guilty of a sinful behavior. We do them a terrible injustice if we excuse them as not being accountable for their actions due to circumstances we say are just beyond their control. This can prevent them from looking for the root cause of their involvement in the first place. It is because of the pleasure they desire; that is the root cause of most of these types of problems.

We are told about this problem in the book of Hebrews; 11:25–26; "He chose to be mistreated along with the people of

God rather than to enjoy the pleasures of sin for a short time. He regarded disgrace for the sake of Christ as of greater value than the treasures of Egypt, because he was looking ahead to his reward." It is a sad fact, but we must remember that the consequences of our sins last much longer than the pleasures we gain from them; they will last forever, unless you ask God to forgive you for them and repent.

So many people have been lead astray after they find themselves "in over their heads" in these types of sinful activities. They are not being told how they have created their problems through their sinful lifestyles; they are told it is an addiction, so it is not their fault. Man has been excusing his wrongful behavior since the time Adam and Eve committed the first sin; it's nothing new. We should help those suffering from addictions to understand why they are by explaining about the God-shaped hole they are trying to fill with these thrill-seeking activities. If they are made to understand the reality of their condition, they have a much better chance of overcoming it.

These individuals must be made to see their condition as self-induced, so they can accept responsibility for their own actions. Then they can see their need for help with the root cause, rather than just trying to deal with the aftermath of the activities. When they see the whole picture, they can recognize their sinful nature, and the Holy Spirit can convict them of their sin. The heart of their solution is to recognize their sinful state, and being lead to repentance and salvation. Every Christian should be sharing about our need for salvation. Candy-coating sinful behavior and giving it a new definition as some type of illness or genetic trait will help no one. Sin is sin; it always has been, and it always will be!

If you are someone who is involved in some of these types

of activities which leave you spent and at your wits' end, look inward for the root cause of your condition. Do not let anyone convince you of being exempt from accountability because whatever ails you is beyond your control. When someone tells you what God's Word says about such conditions as these, do not feel they are not being compassionate towards you; they are being much more compassionate than someone who makes excuses for you. God's Word says in Romans 10:14–15:

> How, then, can they call on the one they have not believed in? And how can they believe in the one of whom they have not heard? And how can they hear without someone preaching to them? And how can they preach unless they are sent? As it is written, "How beautiful are the feet of those who bring good news!"

The man or woman who shares the "good news" of salvation with you, which can free you from your life of bondage to any sinful activity which enslaves you, is the most caring person you will ever meet! When you have seen the difference between excusing your sinful activities and being convicted of them, you will ask God to forgive you. You will also thank whoever helped you to understand that difference. Until you realize this difference, you have no chance of overcoming your sinful habits. You can take medications, attend seminars, join self-help groups, or try any other method society recommends for people suffering as you are. Try what you like, but without your acceptance of the fact you are ultimately responsible for your own behavior, you will not seek help from the only one who can give it to you—God.

I Have a Different Religion

In their attempts to fill the "God-shaped hole" in their hearts, another thing people try instead of Christianity are other religions of the world. There are too many alternative religions out there for me to name them all, but all of these religions share something in common: they are all trying to fill this God-shaped hole we have been talking about. They all teach different means to get there, but in the end, all religions try to reach some form of heaven. Some say the only way for men to reach heaven is to keep improving until he is finally good enough to enter paradise. Some say this may not even be possible in only one lifetime, so the concept of reincarnation was thought up. Your soul may be placed into several different bodies to continually make improvement on itself, until you can finally reach the point of acceptability for entry into whatever form of paradise you might want to believe exists.

Some religions say to reach utopia, you simply must die in battle serving your religion. Some say you must become an agnostic in your spirit by not caring about anything in this life; then you are qualified to enter the massive space which makes up the heavens. This state of "nothingness" is compared to becoming a drop of water which enters the ocean. You become a part of the whole, and lose all individuality. There are many different types of heavens and paradises contained in these alternative religions, and just as many ways of reaching them.

It may seem overly simplistic to group all of these religions together, but that is the beauty of Christianity. God's Word was not written so that only the highly educated would be able to understand it. Sometimes, they are the ones who actually have the most difficulty understanding it. Jesus told us about this fact in Matthew 11:25–26; "At that time Jesus said, 'I praise you, Father, Lord of heaven and earth, because you have hidden these things from the wise and learned, and revealed them to little children. Yes, Father, for this was your good pleasure.'" It was Christians who Jesus was referring to as "little children." He was not referring to infants; He was referring to the "little children" of God.

It can be very difficult for a person who is highly educated by the secular world to accept the Bible as the authoritative Word of God. They believe man's knowledge is the ultimate authority on any given subject, and reject the notion of an all-knowing, all-powerful Creator of the Universe who inspired a book of Ultimate Truth.

Turning to God's Book of Truth, the Bible, we read from John 14:6; "Jesus answered, 'I am the way and the truth and the life. No one comes to the Father except through me.'" Jesus declared this to us, and we must disagree with any alternative men come up with to dispute this fact.

Many people in this modern world want to call Christians exclusive, bigoted, and narrow-minded. We need to remember that it wasn't us who made this statement which offends so many; it was our Lord Jesus Christ! To deny this truth is to deny the one who stated it—something we cannot and must not do! It is one of the fundamental truths of our Bible. The only way to renew the fellowship with God which was lost when Adam and Eve committed the original sin is through the acceptance of the gift offered through Jesus' death on the Cross. God's Word offers no other path to this fellowship with God, so any alternative must be denied if you are going to call yourself a Christian who follows God's principles as laid out in His Word.

Today, we are seeing many events which are being called

multi-religious or multi-cultural due to the fact they are trying to blend many different religious speakers together for some forum in a united front against some social ill or condition. We should not have a problem with uniting people from different backgrounds for a good cause, but we should have a problem with so-called Christian leaders who claim that all religions are merely using different methods to get to the same place. This is a direct contradiction to what Jesus states throughout the Gospels. This view is called a pluralistic one which says: all roads may lead in different directions, but they all end up in the same place. To believe other religions are worshipping the same God and lead to the same Heaven, is to completely ignore the teaching found in the Bible.

There are so many references to Christ being the only way to reach the Father; you must dismiss or ignore them entirely in order to believe otherwise. Do not allow yourself to mistakenly believe this pluralistic view is compatible with the Christian one; it cannot be. If you are going to call yourself a Christian, you must accept the sovereignty of our Lord Jesus Christ.

God's Word says Jesus Christ is the only one who can lead us to heaven. Because Christian ministers are willing to stand up and preach this from their pulpits, the world calls us bigoted and closed-minded. Men of this age do not want to hear the truth of the Scriptures because it convicts them of their sinful lifestyles. They seek out individuals from different religions and beliefs who offer them a more easily accepted alternative. Some are looking for something allowing them to live out their lives doing whatever their carnal nature desires, but still promising them a reward in their afterlife. Others are looking for a religion which tells them they will be rewarded for the things they do for the religion itself. Still others are looking for alternatives teaching whatever we do or say in life is irrelevant, because God will forgive us out of the goodness of his heart regardless of our lifestyles. They are looking for reinforcement that it's okay to participate in activities which the Bible calls sinful, and that they will still be spared from God's wrath because of His love.

This is nothing new. Man has been doing this same thing since Christ's death on the Cross. We can read in 2 Timothy 4:2–5:

> Preach the Word; be prepared in season and out of season; correct, rebuke and encourage—with great patience and careful instruction. For the time will come when men will not put up with sound doctrine. Instead, to suit their own desires, they will gather around them a great number of teachers to say what their itching ears want to hear. They will turn their ears away from the truth and turn aside to myths. But you, keep your head in all situations, endure hardship, do the work of an evangelist, discharge all the duties of your ministry.

This was the Apostle Paul's instructions for a young preacher named Timothy. He was warning him about how the people will get to the point where they will not listen to the sound doctrine as given by God in His Word. Men will assemble together and choose what they want to hear, and to whom they shall listen. This is the case men are making today, and their itching ears have turned them away from hearing the truth of the Scriptures. It is only through the efforts of men of God who are willing to preach the Word as it is written that many of us have a chance to come to our salvation. If doing so causes them to be labeled as bigots and exclusionary, that is what they will have to be called.

We can read about how Jesus promised this would happen in the book of John 15:18–21:

> If the world hates you, keep in mind that it hated me first. If you belonged to the world, it would love you as its own. As it is, you do not belong to the world, but I have chosen you out of the world. That is why the world hates you. Remember the words I spoke to you: No servant is greater than his master. If they persecuted me, they will persecute you also. If they obeyed my teaching, they will obey yours also. They will treat you this way because of my name, for they do not know the One who sent me.

If you are reading this book out of curiosity, but you know in your heart you are not a believer of Christ yet; I implore you to obtain a Bible and read it for yourself. Even if you aren't a believer, you can ask God to help you as you read His Word. Ask Him to send His Spirit to help you understand what is written there. Pray for Him to open your eyes and soften your heart so you may see and feel what is there for you.

We are told in Romans 10:17; "Consequently, faith comes from hearing the message, and the message is heard through the word of Christ." Reading is a form of hearing, so if you read the Scriptures, you will hear the Word of God. When God speaks to you, you will see the error of any other path you have chosen on this earth. This will not make you a bigot; it will make you a child of God! Then you will begin to understand why the world's religions choose to battle against Christianity, and you will feel compassion for the people of this world who have not heard God's Word in a way that meant something to them yet.

I'm an Atheist

Another choice people make which denies Christianity is to claim they are non-religious people who are known as atheists. There are many people who claim to be atheists, but most of them who make this claim are actually not. To truly believe there is no God is a very difficult thing to do. Claiming to believe this is easy; believing is not. Many people who claim to be atheists use it as a defense mechanism to avoid conversations which are spiritual in nature. This can be a very effective way to stop someone in their tracks when they are trying to share the "good news" of the Gospel, so it is used often with that objective in mind.

To be a *true* atheist takes just as much faith as it does to be a believer in God, if not more. We can read in Romans 1:18–20:

> The wrath of God is being revealed from Heaven against all the godlessness and wickedness of men who suppress the truth by their wickedness, since what may be known about God is plain to them, because God has made it plain to them. For since the creation of the world God's invisible qualities—his eternal power and divine nature—have been clearly seen, being understood from what has been made, so that men are without excuse.

This statement made by the Apostle Paul makes it very clear that men should see God's reality simply by observing the things He has created. We should observe the heavens and the earth, the wonders of this planet, and all the creatures which inhabit it; including man. If you just take the time to consider the intricate designs God used in His creation, you cannot help but see the hand of the Master in His work. I do not mean you need to see places like the Grand Canyon, Yellowstone National Parks, Mt. Everest, or any of the other "wonders of the world." I mean if you just look at the majesty existing in your own backyard, you should be able to see the beauty God placed into His creation.

If you just take the time to notice the majesty in all of creation, you will not be able to credit it all to some chance occurrence; you will know that God was behind it all. In our modern times, there is a debate raging over the mere mention of what is called the "intelligent design" theory of creation. Most supporters of this theory do not even put a name to the "designer;" they just want to suggest the possibility one must exist. Allowing this to be taught in our schools would undermine the very strategy of removing God from the education system, so it is no wonder we see the amount of resistance which has been mounted against any such teaching.

Personally, I believe—short of God performing a miraculous turnaround in our public education system—He will never be allowed back into it again. In our beginning, God and the Bible formed the very foundations for our educational system, but secular society has succeeded in removing them both. This means to educate our children about God, we have to do it at home, church, and in private schools. We need to take warning, because these institutions are being attacked as well by those who promote the world's view. It is only a matter of time before they are going to be as passionately maligned on this subject as the public school system already has been.

So when you look at what it takes to be an atheist, you can see how it takes great faith to deny the reality of God, when all of His creation shouts His very existence! But if you have yourself convinced you are truly an atheist, I can offer this advice: look carefully at the world around you and search your heart. I hear you saying you don't believe in God, but go ahead and ask Him to talk to your heart just in case He really does exist; what have you got to lose? When you look at the intricacies and the beauty which exists in nature, you will know they didn't "just happen." Although they don't put a name on the designer in the "intelligent design" theory, they at least acknowledge His existence. This could be your first step towards salvation, so I cannot urge you to take it strongly enough. As we read from Romans, you will be "without excuse" when you stand before God, solely from these facts of creation; so do not dismiss them, embrace them and believe.

2

Why Aren't Christians Reaching the Unsaved?

More Excuses

Chapter Nine

The Church is Sending Mixed Signals

I have tried to understand why so many people are not being lead to Christ through His church and His followers, and I will share what I believe are some of the reasons I have found in this second half of this book. By no means will I be covering them all, but I will share what I have discovered. I have asked the Holy Spirit to open my eyes to see clearly, and to reveal things which were hidden from my understanding. It proved to be a simple task to uncover the many excuses people use for dismissing Christ from their lives. In most cases, I had used many of these excuses myself in my past. The first to turn to is the Church itself, and we will look at the many different signals we hear from it. It is easy to see this situation exists, and the world helps to perpetuate this condition. The "Christian Church" is sending out many different messages, and that comes as no surprise when you consider the many different beliefs which are incorporated under this title. The secular world is pushing the agenda of inclusiveness in the Church, and this helps lead to the many mixed signals people are receiving.

In the eyes of the world, any church that follows a deity known as God is considered to be a Christian one. This can be observed by noticing events put together where a collection of different types of churches are gathered together into a hodgepodge which is called a multi-denominational event. I am not talking about mixing denominations with slightly different views; I am talking about putting together events where you may hear a Baptist preacher speak, followed by a Muslim cleric.

The world is pushing this condition with great effort, and it is called being inclusive in your religious thinking. You may feel there is nothing sinister about such a position, but if you look deeper into what is happening, you can see the dangerous results which can come out of these events. At the very least, the fundamental Christian Church is allowing themselves to be blended into this hodgepodge, and are being used to lend credibility to the other religious groups present. You find Christian, Muslim, Hindu, and many other religious speakers at these events. You can also find self-help and motivational speakers at these events, which serves as an implication of their being as beneficial as the clergymen present.

Any protests against these "blended" events tend to come from fundamental Christians who don't believe other religious beliefs should be mixed with their own. Protests never seem to come from the other groups demanding that Christianity not be allowed to share with their gatherings. Quite the contrary, we find Christian gatherings, advertised as traditional values types of meetings, being challenged by groups like the A.C.L.U. in an attempt to force their inclusive agenda upon them.

These attacks against Christian organizations use a two-pronged approach by demanding inclusion of various other groups, and then denouncing the Christian faith as being exclusionary. These non-Christian groups, being championed by the A.C.L.U., do not even have to be religious in content. They may be some group advocating a particular agenda such as homosexual marriages or environmental protection. There seems to be no limitation placed on groups challenging the exclusiveness of a fundamental Christian gathering; the doors have been thrown wide open to all comers.

The world has placed Christianity into a catch-twenty-two position; we can't win for losing. Because Christianity wants to remain autonomous so as not to allow our message to be watered down by opposing views, the media proclaims our position as being bigoted. The confusion generated by this mixing of several different religious ideologies is wreaking havoc in the minds of the unsaved. When you have ministers of Christian faiths sharing a podium with non-Christian leaders, it grants them a place of legitimacy and significance, resulting in this confusion.

We need to listen to the words spoken by Jesus which are found in John 14:6; "Jesus answered, I am the way and the truth and the life. No one comes to the Father except through me." This is one of the most fundamental of Biblical doctrines! Jesus is the one and only way to reach our Father in Heaven. He said so, and if you are going to call yourself a Christian, you must believe it! Jesus Himself stated the exclusivity of His deity; the church did not say it for Him. This means when someone calls you a bigot for believing in Christ, it is Jesus who they are really referring to. He is the one who taught this truth, and He said there was no other way to get into Heaven. He did not worry about being "politically correct." He simply stated the truth, as declared by His Father in Heaven.

Another passage we should look at is John 3:16–18:

> For God so loved the world that he gave his one and only Son, that whoever believes in him shall not perish but have eternal life. For God did not send his Son into the world to condemn the world, but to save the world through him. Whoever believes in him is not condemned, but whoever does not believe stands condemned already because he has not believed in the name of God's one and only Son.

This passage is another example of Christ's claim to being the exclusive Son of God. This particular passage takes it to an even higher level, by telling us not only is Jesus the only way to reach Heaven, it also tells us if we choose not to believe in Him; we are already condemned and cannot reach Heaven because of our unbelief. To deny Jesus Christ as the one and only way into Heaven is to deny Him as your Lord and Savior. As true followers of Christ, we cannot give the impression to the ungodly that there is another ideology worthy of their consideration. This is exactly what happens when you mix completely different religious and secular organizations together into one gathering. It is like combining ingredients into a blender, and mixing them until they all become lost in the same concoction.

This occurrence of multi-religious events is fairly new in our society, but the purpose behind them is not. Man has always tried to find ways to deny the deity of Christ, so he could continue living as he wants without feeling guilt for his sinful lifestyle. We were warned this condition would become a reality in 2 Timothy 4:2–5:

> Preach the Word; be prepared in season and out of season; correct, rebuke and encourage—with great patience and careful instruction. For the time will come when men will not put up with sound doctrine. Instead, to suit their own desires, they will gather around them a great number of teachers to say what their itching ears want to hear. They will turn their ears away from the truth and turn aside to myths. But you, keep your head in all situations, endure hardship, do the work of an evangelist, discharge all the duties of your ministry.

This stern and prophetic warning was given by the Apostle Paul to a young preacher named Timothy. Paul knew this was the position man would take, and it is the position the world has taken today. Using this method of mixing many different religious beliefs together into one format is simply a new way of trying to accomplish this objective. The goal is to present the Christian view as just one of many possible ways leading to Heaven, and to portray Christians as bigots for refusing to be "politically correct." This has done so much damage to those who are unsaved, because it confuses them to the point that they don't know what to believe, and this often appears to be the overall objective of those bringing the accusations.

So what is the solution to this problem? It is a simple one: do not submit to the mixing of religions into a mess of blended misunderstandings and misinterpretations. Christian churches need to stand their ground, and not give in to the pressures the world is putting on them to lower the standards which Jesus set for us in the Scriptures. If holding to these principles established by God means your church is going to be criticized by the secular world, so be it. This is nothing new, because we were told it would happen in John 15:18–21:

> If the world hates you, keep in mind that it hated me first. If you belonged to the world, it would love you as its own. As it is, you do not belong to the world, but I have chosen you out of the world. That is why the world hates you. Remember the words I spoke to you: No servant is greater than his master. If they persecuted me, they will persecute you also. If they obeyed my teaching, they will obey yours also. They will treat you this way because of my name, for they do not know the One who sent me.

Jesus gave us the answer to whether or not His Church should give in to the pressures of the world, and water down His teaching. He told us we would be persecuted for following His way, and we are. This persecution serves as proof we are following His directions, because we were told we would be persecuted for believing in Him as Lord and Savior. Although it is not pleasant to suffer these types of persecution, it is a joy to know you are being abused just because of your faith in Christ. That is the message we are taught in James 1:2–3; "Consider it pure joy, my brothers, whenever you face trials of many kinds, because you know that the testing of your faith develops perseverance."

So when we look for an answer to this mixing of religions into a common arena, it is easy to find in God's Word, but painful to initiate. We know we will be persecuted for proclaiming the exclusivity of Christ's deity, but we must. Stand firm, and do not waiver in this trial in which we find ourselves. Do not allow yourselves to be used by the world in its efforts to minimize the significance of Christianity through the legitimizing of other worldly religions and ideologies. This is the exact opposite of what we are called to do. We need to continue proclaiming the truth of Jesus' position as the author and finisher of our faith, and His identity as the one and only Son of God.

He is the only one who can justify us, and we must not allow ourselves to be used in any way to make it more difficult for the unsaved to come to the saving knowledge of this fact. That means standing firm in the truths which God placed in the Bible for us to follow. One of the most fundamental of these is found in Acts 4:12; "Salvation is found in no one else, for there is no other name under Heaven given to men by which we must be saved." No other name. That is exclusivity!

This mixing different religions and ideologies into common forums at special events and gatherings is merely the next logical step in the blending process which has been underway for some time in our society. The secular world has been working at this process for a very long time, and this was just the natural next step. The next thing for us to do is to look into the methods used in this mixing bowl theology. To do this, we will look at the many different types of religious organizations our society groups together under the heading *Christianity*.

We will place the one Church which we shall call the true Christian Church, on the top of this list. There are many different denominations under this heading, with many slight differences between each. It may be in the way they perform the Sacraments of Baptism or Communion. It may be in the different types of hymns they sing during church services. Other differences may be in the views they take on infant Baptism vs. Dedication services, or the days on which their services take place. It may be in the particular translation they use as their Bible of choice. Another difference may be that some have women in places of authority while others may not. Different styles of apparel their clergy and congregations wear during their services can be another difference. Some clergy will be in suit and tie, others will be dressed casually; still others may wear flowing robes. Some congregations will have men wearing suits and ties and the women in dresses, while others have men dressed casually and women wearing pants. Many congregations have a mix of both, and members wear whatever they feel most comfortable in on any given day of services.

There are many slight differences to be found between different denominations of the Christian church. It is the significance of particular differences we must examine more closely to understand what separates any of these different denominations from each other, versus separating them from what should be called the Christian Church. If we use the standards established by the world, we find there is such a wide range of accepted ideologies, it is difficult to determine what a Christian Church really is. However, if we look to Scripture and use the standards God established through His written Word, it is much easier to determine whether or not a particular religious denomination should be considered as part of the overall Christian Church.

These standards which God has established in His Word are called doctrinal truths. There are numerous doctrines presented in Scripture. We will look at some describing the requirements any church must accept in order to be qualified as part of our Lord Jesus Christ's Church. Our first such doctrine is located at the very beginning of Scripture, in the book of Genesis 1:1; "In the beginning, God created the heavens and the earth."

This verse is an excellent example of truth as it is found in Scripture. Look at the first statement in this verse; "In the beginning, God..." God was there at the very beginning. There is no mention of others; there is only God. He was there at the beginning, and then we see the second half of this verse; "...God created the heavens and the earth." It is there for all to see if we just but read the Bible; God created the heavens and the earth. The universe did not evolve out of some mass of particles which collected together in the far reaches of space. Earth did not appear out of the total mass in some haphazard manner; it appeared when God created it.

This passage serves as a good example of what is called a doctrinal truth. In order for any religious organization to qualify as a Christian church, they must believe the truth of all Biblical doctrines. If you are attending a church that does not teach creation as told in God's Word, it is not a fundamental Christian church. It is simple to determine whether or not your church is following the true teaching of God. Just read His Word for yourself, and see if they teach in agreement with what is there.

There are many doctrinal truths found throughout Scripture which form the basic building blocks of the Christian Church. One of them, which serves as the very cornerstone of our faith, is found in Matthew 16:13–16:

> When Jesus came to the region of Caesarea Philippi, He asked His disciples, "Who do people say the Son of Man is?" They replied, "Some say John the Baptist; others say Elijah; and still others, Jeremiah or one of the prophets." "But what about you?" He asked. "Who do you say I am?" Simon Peter answered, "You are the Christ, the Son of the living God."

This is one of the most fundamental truths from God's Word: Jesus Christ is the one and only Son of the living God. If the place where you choose to worship does not follow this doctrine, it is not following God's Word. It doesn't matter if they include the name of Christ in their title, or whatever else they may do to imply they are Christian in nature. If they do not teach Jesus Christ as the Son of God, they are not a Christian church. Jesus Christ was not just a good teacher, He was not just a prophet, and He was not just a rebel who changed the world. He was, is, and will always be the Son of God! In order for any denomination to qualify as Christian they must teach this truth, and you must believe it to become a Christian.

One doctrine which takes this one step further in defining what is required of us in order to be Christian, is found in Acts 4:12; "Salvation is found in no one else, for there is no other name under Heaven given by which we must be saved." We find here that not only is Jesus the one and only Son of the living God, but He is also the only one through whom we can be saved. There is no other name by which we can be saved; none whatsoever. So, if your denomination teaches that there is any sort of alternative leading to salvation, they are not following God's Word. If they teach that you need Christ plus anything else, they are not being true to God's Word. There is no other possible route to Heaven; Jesus is the only way! This is another Biblical truth we must believe in our hearts in order to be saved.

A common practice many churches participate in is adding to or leaving out some portion of God's Word in their teaching. It can manifest itself through their teaching on these doctrines in a way only presenting a partial view of them. They may leave out portions which stand out as contradictions to the ideologies which are taught in their services. They also may add to Scripture, by insinuating there is more to them than what is plainly there for all to see, if we would just read for ourselves. Because some churches wander from what is written, it becomes even more important for us to spend time in reading God's Word for ourselves.

To illustrate the importance of reading God's Word on your own, turn to Deuteronomy 11:16–21:

> Be careful, or you will be enticed to turn away and worship other gods and bow down to them. Then the Lord's anger will burn against you, and He will shut the Heavens so that it will not rain and the ground will yield no produce, and you will soon perish from the good land the Lord is giving you. Fix these words of mine in your hearts and minds; tie them as symbols on your hands and bind them on your foreheads. Teach them to your children, talking about them when you sit at home and when you walk along the road, when you lie down and when you get up. Write them on the doorframes of your houses and on your gates, so that your days and the days of your children may be many in the land that the Lord swore to give your forefathers, as many as the days that the Heavens are above the earth.

Here, we plainly see the importance of reading and meditating on the Scriptures for our own good, so we will not be enticed to turn away from the one true God and worship some other false god. If we fall victim to this, His anger will burn against us. We are told to place God's Word into our hearts, so we will not forget it. It is to be burned into our minds, and we are to teach our children to do the same. We need to remember the Scriptures when we lay down, and when we get up. They are to be placed on the doorframes of our homes so all who pass by will know we follow God's Word.

God told us to read His Word for ourselves because there is always the danger of another individual leading us astray if we rely completely on someone else's guidance to learn what the Bible has to say. Many of us simply fail to follow this command, and that is a large part of the reason why churches that are teaching doctrine contrary to the Word of God are able to exist. If you prayerfully read what is there in your Bible, you will be able to tell whether or not your church is following the truths that are there.

Another doctrine many churches leave out of their teaching is the doctrine of sin. God's Word teaches about what is called "original sin" which means the first sin ever committed by mankind. We already looked at this earlier, and found it written in the third chapter of the book of Genesis. It is the account of the fall of man as he was tempted by the serpent in the Garden of Eden. Eve, the first woman, succumbed to the serpent's pleading with her to challenge the authority of God by eating the fruit of the forbidden tree, which held the knowledge of good and evil. After she had done so, Adam was easily convinced to follow her lead. By this one act, sin entered the world, and every human has been subject to it since.

If your church does not teach the world as sinless before this downfall, they are not following God's Word. In the same way, they must teach that mankind began with this first couple: Adam and Eve. If in any way whatsoever, your church denies the account of creation as found in Genesis, they are not teaching Christianity. They cannot imply that God used evolution as His means of creating life, or say the timetable listed in Genesis is not the correct one. Examples like this which add to or take away from doctrinal truth as found in Scripture, are exactly what Scripture warns us about. If you find yourself in a church guilty of this practice, then find yourself a new one which teaches the whole Word of God.

Looking at another doctrine involving sin, we can turn to Romans 3:23; "For all have sinned, and fall short of the glory of God." This verse is short and straight to the point; all have sinned. There has been no human born who has not sinned, other than the one and only Son of God. We are born into sin, and we live our lives in sin. All of us find ourselves guilty, in this respect, without exception. We all fall short of God's glory. It is the reason why we need salvation, because we are sinful men and women who cannot see God in our sinful states.

To look deeper into this sinful state, we need to understand the consequences for us because of this sinful nature. They are found in Romans 6:23; "For the wages of sin is death, but the gift of God is eternal life in Christ Jesus our Lord." Here, we are told quite vividly what the outcome of our sin will be; death. But we are also told we have available to us the gift of eternal life through Jesus Christ!

Once we have read these passages of Scripture, we must put our understanding of them into practical use. If your church is not teaching these truths just as they are found in Scripture, they are not following God's Word. They must teach their congregations that we are all guilty of sin. They must teach us about the punishment for our sin, which will be death unless we allow Jesus to save us from this fate awaiting all sinners. They must teach Jesus Christ as the only way we can be saved, or they are teaching falsely.

It can be quite simple to determine whether or not your church is teaching Christianity as found in the Bible. We just have to read the Scriptures for ourselves to find what is there, and then put our church's teaching to the test. It will not be hard to see if they pass or fail this test. The more doctrines you examine and use in your testing, the easier it becomes to make a determination. With that thought in mind, let's look at one of the most fundamental of all Biblical doctrines; the manner by which salvation comes to us.

To examine this, we need to look at Ephesians 2:1–5, 8–9:

> As for you, you were dead in your transgressions and sins, in which you used to live when you followed the ways of this world and of the ruler of the kingdom of the air, the spirit who is now at work in those who are disobedient. All of us also lived among them at one time, gratifying the cravings of our sinful nature and following its desires and thoughts. Like the rest, we were by nature objects of wrath. But because of His great love for us, God, who is rich in mercy, made us alive with Christ even when we were dead in transgressions—it is by grace you have been saved.
>
> For it is by grace you have been saved, through faith—and this not from yourselves, it is the gift of God—not by works, so that no one can boast.

This doctrine of salvation by grace through faith in Jesus Christ is one of the most crucial to the Christian faith. It is sometimes misunderstood, and many times it is taught in a manner not following what is clearly stated in this passage. Because this truth is so important for all of us, we must take all the time necessary to understand it. I cannot express to you strongly enough the importance of reading it prayerfully for yourselves. If you read it in this manner, the Holy Spirit can reveal the truth directly to you; so please, give Him the opportunity.

We have already established that Jesus is our only way to Heaven, and He is the one and only Son of the living God. The next thing we need to understand is what we must do to receive this gift of eternal life. This piece of the puzzle is found in Romans 10:9–11:

> That if you confess with your mouth, 'Jesus is Lord,' and believe in your heart that God raised Him from the dead, you will be saved. For it is with your heart that you believe and are justified, and it is with your mouth that you confess and are saved. As the Scripture says, 'Anyone who trusts in Him will never be put to shame.'

In this passage of Scripture, we have one of the most crucial doctrines we can look at to determine whether the place of worship we attend is truly a Christian church, and at the same time, we can look at whether or not we are truly a Christian. We read earlier from the book of Ephesians about how we are saved through grace by faith, and not by works. Now we have read in the book of Romans about how, in order to receive this saving grace, we must accomplish two separate tasks. The first one is simply to profess with our mouth that Jesus is our Lord and Savior, and we usually find this step to be the easier of the two. The second step requires us to believe in our hearts that God raised Him from the dead. This step is the one which many have a lot of difficulty with—the act of believing unconditionally.

It is one of the saddest states men and women can find

themselves in: confessing with their mouths, but not being able to believe in their hearts. They can reach a point where they want to believe so desperately, but fail to do so. I feel their pain, because I suffered under this condition for a long period in my own life. If you find yourself stuck in this perpetual state of wanting to believe, but remaining in doubt, plead your case with Jesus. Pray without ceasing, and He will help you to find your place of salvation.

Now we have seen that having and professing faith in Jesus Christ is our part of this salvation process. When we have fulfilled these requirements, God promises we will be saved through His grace. It is a gift from God, supplied through His Son's dying on the Cross in our place. His Word also says this salvation is eternal; you can never lose it. You can find this truth in John 10:27–30:

> My sheep listen to my voice; I know them, and they follow me. I give them eternal life, and they shall never perish; no one can snatch them out of my hand. My Father, who has given them to me, is greater than all; no one can snatch them out of my Father's hand. I and the Father are one.

We have now read how salvation is a gift from God. It comes to us through the grace of God, as a reward for our believing in faith and confessing His Son's sovereignty. It is eternal; no one, and nothing, can ever take us away from the hand of God after we are truly saved. Jesus is the only way to get to this salvation, because He is the one and only Son of God. Now, let's look at the closing thought from what we read earlier in Ephesians, telling us this gift comes from grace, and not from any works we have done, in case we might find reason to boast.

To look at this subject of "works," first we need to understand that "works" simply means the things which we do in our lives. It can mean the activities we participate in, such as church projects. It can also just mean the workings we do in our minds. The thoughts we have, and the ways that we live because of these thoughts, are examples of the works which we perform during our lifetimes. People can go astray in this area, by falsely believing in any way whatsoever, that their works can have some influence on whether or not they will receive salvation. This is a contradiction to the doctrine of saving grace by faith as a gift from God, and I sympathize with those who stumble in this area; I did too for many years.

It is easy to become confused in this doctrine, because in our minds it makes sense to "do" something, in order to receive God's gift. At the very least, we should have to clean up our act and become more "righteous." But we can never become righteous in the eyes of God, because we continue to live in sin. It's hard for us to accept this notion of not being able to do anything to help ourselves; but, accept it we must. Only after you accept this fact, will you be able to rely on God's grace alone for your salvation. If you continue in the belief that you can somehow influence God through your own efforts, you will never make the spiritual progress you should.

There are two passages which shed some light on this subject. One of them is found in James 2:14–17:

> What good is it, my brothers, if a man claims to have faith but has no deeds? Can such faith save him? Suppose a brother or sister is without clothes and daily food. If one of you says to him, 'Go, I wish you well; keep warm and well fed,' but does nothing about his

> physical needs, what good is it? In the same way, faith by itself, if it is not accompanied by action, is dead.

We see through this passage, how our deeds and actions are of much worth, but are not determining factors in our salvation. Our deeds and actions should shine much brighter because of the faith within us, but they do not have to shine in order to receive our faith. We should strive to live as Christ did, and through this effort, we will perform deeds to help others. We cannot become convinced our deeds and actions determine whether or not we were saved in the first place; they had nothing to do with it. Our deeds and actions just serve as proofs of the faith inside of us; not as the factors which brought that faith to us.

The second of these two passages deals with this matter in a slightly different way, and is found in 1 John 3:2–3; "Dear friends, now we are children of God, and what we will be has not yet been made known. But we know that when He appears, we shall be like Him, for we shall see Him as He is. Everyone who has this hope in him purifies himself, just as He is pure." Once someone has this hope of salvation inside of them, they should undergo a process of purification. This is called sanctification, and through it we will become more righteous, by following our guidance from the Holy Spirit. After receiving our gift of salvation, we should strive to become holier than we are in our present state. This should be a continual process, and we won't reach our final state of perfection, called glorification, until we are in Heaven. This sanctification process is another natural transition to follow after we have been saved, and has nothing to do with whether or not we are saved; salvation is by the grace of God alone.

Now we have seen a sampling of Biblical doctrines we can

use to determine whether or not our church is following God's Word in their teaching. We know God was here from the beginning. We know He created the Heavens and the earth. We know He created mankind in the persons of Adam and Eve. We know original sin entered through their falling to the temptation of the serpent. We know all have sinned since, except for the one and only Son of God. We know the only way to receive our salvation comes from believing in Christ. We know it is a gift of God, and by His grace alone. We know we can do nothing through deeds and actions to influence whether or not we are saved. We also know if we do not receive this gift of salvation, we will suffer death and eternal punishment through separation from God. We know the only way to receive this gift is through the name of Jesus Christ. When we put these doctrines together, we can determine if a church is teaching them properly or not. All you have to do is take the time to prayerfully read God's Word, and these doctrinal truths will jump out at you. They are there for all to see if we just make the effort to see them; so make that effort!

While you are considering what your church teaches, you can also look at what you believe personally. Becoming aware of these truths found in the Scriptures provides an opportunity for self-examination. Do you believe in the truth of these doctrines? If not, you need to determine what it is you do believe, and why. There is nothing as important as our salvation, so do not put off making this assessment of yourself. Not only is the life we live on earth going to be determined by our beliefs, but also our possibility of having an eternal life with God in Heaven.

When you take the time to look at the different churches and religious organizations which the world classifies as Christian, you will find many that are not following these fundamental doctrines from God's Word. Some may appear to be Christian in most of what they teach, but stray on one or more points. They cannot wander away from any of these doctrines in the Scriptures, and still be truly Christian in their teaching. If they do not accept all that is written in the Bible as the infallible Word of God, they are not teaching the truth of Christian principles to their congregations.

The secular world is quick to pour as many different belief systems into one melting pot as they can possibly manage. This is because it fits the agenda the world has of belittling our God and His Word. It is why the world justifies giving the title of Christian to numerous people who live a life far removed from the principles laid down in Scripture. The purpose for this is to convince as many unsaved people as possible that they don't need to consider Christianity for their lives, since they are already just like those who call themselves Christians. This is one of the most successful tactics satan has used throughout history.

There are denominations trying to justify their nonconformance to Biblical doctrines by stating they have found a new and modern interpretation of the Scriptures. They use the devices of the world to justify their own methods of understanding; devices such as scientific studies which try to disprove doctrines which have been accepted since the beginning of Christianity. A good example of this type of defiance is found in the way the world is struggling to re-write God's Word about the area of homosexuality.

God's Word teaches us about individuals who have sexual relations with members of the same sex. It is called a sinful behavior, and is condemned in many passages of Scripture. Yet, in many so-called Christian churches today, homosexuality is viewed as acceptable behavior and is endorsed through performing unions and marriages between same-sex couples. Some of these churches even allow habitual offenders to be ordained as ministers and priests. The world claims scientific evidence has proven that homosexuality is a trait people have in their genes, and therefore they have no choice in their sexual orientation. These types of claims are nothing new; they are just one more attempt by men to justify their own sinful nature.

These attacks against God's truth are why it is so important to read the Scriptures for ourselves. If you become familiar with them, then you can determine whether or not any church is teaching the truth, some artificial half-truth, or straight out lies—passing them off as Christianity to their congregations. To fail to teach the whole truth, places all those who follow your teaching in jeopardy. In the example of homosexuality, to teach people it is acceptable is to deny that God has called it sinful. These individuals then fail to see their sin, and are not led to their need for repentance. Without repentance, there can be no forgiveness. This is why it is so important for Christian churches to preach the whole Word of God without exceptions. Men and women are led to salvation by the truth found in Scripture, not by twisting or denying those truths.

We can see another way that secular society is infiltrating their services even in the churches which are teaching Biblical principles as found in Scripture. The infiltration is happening through the church's watering-down of the Scriptures in order to make them more palatable for the public. This is a fairly new method of operating a church, and is called being seeker-friendly in their style of bringing the message to a congregation. Many do not like this title of seeker-friendly, but it has been used to describe this new style of preaching, so it is the one I will use.

One of the characteristics found in these types of churches, is that they tend to choose specific truths to teach while picking others to overlook. The doctrines which tend to bring an uplifting spirit to our souls are taught with great vigor, but those which are meant to convict us of our sinful ways tend to be avoided. Teaching in this manner makes people comfortable with who they are, and avoids making them feel miserable by challenging their sinful lifestyles. This is dangerous, because no one should feel comfortable if they are still living a sinful lifestyle.

When you look at your church's style of teaching, this condition is one you should be watching out for. Does your pastor speak on doctrines from the Scripture, but stop short of pronouncing judgments on those who are guilty of sinful living? Does he always preach on subjects which allow him to maintain a smiling demeanor, instead of subjects which will require a look of resolve? Does he make you feel you will be all right, no matter how you are living your life? These are the characteristics which can be associated with these so-called seeker-friendly churches. It is how they entice new seekers into their congregation, and how they keep the ones already there. It can be a method of making you feel good about yourself, but refraining from telling you that you can never be good enough on your own.

In some churches, this style of teaching may be hard to notice. It is not always easily detected, unless you spend enough time with them to see the pattern present in their teaching. All Christian churches are meant to be seeker-friendly in trying to lead the lost to Christ, but not through making them feel good about themselves regardless of their true conditions. In many churches, it may be a fine line between being evangelical in their methods of bringing new converts into the church, and being seeker-friendly by only sharing what they believe are "friendly" Scriptures with their congregations. There is a difference between these two types of churches, but you will only see the difference if you spend the time required in your own personal Bible study. That is always the best way for us to learn, and the way we are commanded to follow. If you are not doing so, I urge to start today. It is the only way you will know for yourself if your church is teaching the whole Word of God, or if they are teaching with a limitation on it. You may also come to an understanding of whether you are truly a Christian or just an imitation of one. This knowledge can help speed you on your way to the right place for you to worship, and it can help you to get to the right place in your personal walk with Christ.

So do your homework, and spend as much time as possible in the Scriptures. There is nothing you can do on your own that will have as much impact on your life than to study the Word of God. When you spend that time in God's Word, you will gain the ability to see through the counterfeit churches. You will be able to see the true position you hold in your own life, and whether or not you are where God wants you to be. Almost as importantly, you will be able to see where other people are in their lives. This will help you to witness to them, and then maybe you will be used to help lead someone to their salvation.

There is no greater honor we can gain, than to be used in this way. After you have helped someone else to salvation, you will be able to point this new believer to a true, Bible-preaching church—one not watering down the messages taught there, but teaching the whole Word of God, so all who hear it will see their need for repentance and forgiveness. It is our responsibility to reach the point where we can tell the differences between true and untrue Christian churches, so we can help others find where they should go to worship.

Chapter Ten

The Believers Are Sending Mixed Signals

Now that we have looked at the mixed signals being sent out by different churches and religious organizations, we will move on and look at the many different types of individuals who are known as Christians. When we do, we are immediately bombarded by many of the same conditions we found when looking at the various churches the world inclusively classifies as Christian. The world's agenda is present in this category, just as we saw when looking at institutions professing to be Christian, who aren't following the doctrinal truths of God's Word.

To look at the mixed signals sent out by individual believers, we must first see what is required of someone to qualify as a believer. We learned, in the last chapter, how secular society requires very little in order to grant the Christian label to any organization choosing to call itself as such. It seems to take nothing at all to be granted Christian status in our world, and it is the same for any individual who makes this claim. This is because the world wants to demonstrate, to all, that there is no real difference between Christians and non-believers. Calling people Christians, whether they follow Biblical doctrine or not, suits this agenda. That is why our society uses this inclusive manner, regardless of the obvious differences between many individuals and churches.

This inclusiveness has led to many false believers, who not only call themselves Christians, but earnestly believe it to be true. Our society has reinforced their mistaken belief through reassuring them it takes very little, if anything at all, in order to be a Christian. Many of these people do not understand what is required of them to become a believer, because they have become convinced there is nothing required.

This has created a condition of a perpetual state of misunderstanding concerning the Gospel message. The situation arises when an unsaved person begins to search for what is missing in their spiritual life, and they run into someone who professes to be a Christian; but, this professing believer has no real understanding of what they are professing to believe in to begin with. These individuals are useless to the one who is seeking. Even worse, they are usually harmful, because they tend to offer advice on how to become spiritual, without the knowledge to teach. This places one more person into this confused state of misunderstanding about salvation, and then, they go on to repeat the process with others. This has created a never-ending cycle of misunderstanding and misinterpretation of God's Word.

The world is perfectly content to let this situation develop and persist. Society helps this to happen by upholding individuals who gain prominence from the public exposure, and displaying their misguided views for all to see and hear.

This is happening all too often, and is occurring more and more all the time. When a fundamental Christian group brings one of these misguided people to task for their inconsistencies, then the fundamentalist is systematically destroyed by this same media.

There is no litmus test for being a Christian as far as this world is concerned. If you are reading this book because you want to become a believer, but haven't been able to figure out what a believer is, I offer you encouragement as you struggle against this agenda the world has for making it harder for you. I also congratulate you for deciding to fight through the confusion created by all of this deceptive confusion.

Believers are told to help others understand what it means to be a Christian, and we find this written in 1 Peter 3:15–16:

> But in your hearts set apart Christ as Lord. Always be prepared to give an answer to everyone who asks you to give the reason for the hope that you have. But do this with gentleness and respect, keeping a clear conscience, so that those who speak maliciously against your good behavior in Christ may be ashamed of their slander.

I have asked for God's help as I set out to offer an understanding of what it takes to be truly Christian. Some may disagree with the definition I offer, so I urge all of you to earnestly search the Scriptures in order to gain your own understanding. Pray for insight and a discerning mind as you read the passages from God's Word which are used in the following pages, so you may see clearly as you search for God.

To start, I have to stress that there is a huge difference

between being a Christian, and being what the world calls a "religious" person. A religious person, as defined by Webster, is; "an individual who is devoted to a set of religious beliefs or observances." This is one label believers try to avoid as much as possible, but many people continue to place it on us because it is the only one they know. Christians are not just "religious" people in the sense of belonging to a particular church or denomination; we belong to Christ, and the church belongs to Him, too.

I know it can be hard to understand the difference between being a Christian and being religious, because I used to have the same trouble. Being a Christian is about having a relationship with God, not just being part of a church. The "religious" acts we perform while attending a place of worship are a direct result of our relationship with Jesus Christ, and not the other way around. We must never place the church into a position of authority ahead of our Lord, or grant it anywhere near the significance we must place on Him. This is where many religious institutions go wrong, and lead many astray. If any church elevates itself to the level of being able to directly impact your ability to have a relationship with God, they are in denial of the Scriptures.

The two most burning questions I hear when discussing Christianity have always been, "What does it take to become a Christian?", and "What happens to you when you become a Christian?" These are two of the most important questions you can ever ask, and our understanding of them will be a large factor in determining where we will spend our eternity.

When I use the term "Christian," I am referring to a follower of Jesus Christ. They are the only people who will get into Heaven, or who can have a relationship with God. So to start, let's take a look at what it takes to become a Christian.

One thing which must take place to become a Christian was explained to us by Jesus in John 3:3; "In reply Jesus declared, 'I tell you the truth, no one can see the kingdom of God unless he is born again.'"

Jesus was speaking to a religious leader named Nicodemus, who found His statement to be ridiculous. He asked Jesus, "How can a man enter his mother's womb for a second time?" He was thinking in physical terms, while Jesus was speaking in spiritual ones. It is our spirit which must be regenerated, or "born again" in order for us to enter the kingdom of Heaven.

I have met people who profess to be Christians, but say they are not the "born again" type. They have announced their misunderstanding of Scripture, because Christ clearly states you cannot be one without the other. The world has placed a stigma against proclaiming yourself to be a born again believer, because it implies something supernatural has happened to you. As is often the case, whenever the world tries to ridicule and belittle something of the Christian faith, we should pause and look closely, as it is usually a good indication there is something there worth seeing.

God's Word states clearly that if your heart has not been supernaturally regenerated, you have not been spiritually born again. If this is the case in your heart; you are not a Christian. You need to see the truth from this passage in the book of John by looking it up for yourself. If anyone teaches an alternative method for receiving your Christianity, you need to investigate the Scriptures they use to back their belief, just as you should do with the ones I am using. This is something I cannot stress strongly enough; you must do your homework and pray for understanding in order to be sure of what you truly believe.

So what is regeneration, and how does it happen? This

is one of the most important questions anyone can ever ask. It is a supernatural occurrence which changes the spiritual makeup of our hearts and souls when we are born again. We become a completely new individual, as told in 2 Corinthians 5:16–19:

> So from now on we regard no one from a worldly point of view. Though we once regarded Christ in this way, we do so no longer. Therefore, if anyone is in Christ, he is a new creation; the old has gone, the new has come! All this is from God, who reconciled us to himself through Christ and gave us the ministry of reconciliation: that God was reconciling the world to himself in Christ, not counting men's sins against them.

From this passage we see if someone is in Christ, they are not the same person they were before their salvation. Physically, you are the same person, but spiritually, you have been regenerated and have become a new creation. I have heard so many people try to explain what it feels like when you undergo this process, and they are all slightly different from each other. Some people are able to quote the exact date, time, and place where their regeneration occurred. Others say it seemed to happen over a period of time. All agree the most important thing is just having the assurance it has happened.

The Apostle Paul wrote in Philippians 2:12–16;

> Therefore, my dear friends, as you have always obeyed—not only in my presence, but now much more in my absence—continue to work out your salvation with fear and trembling, for it is God who works in you

> to will and to act according to his good purpose. Do everything without complaining or arguing, so that you may become blameless and pure, children of God without fault in a crooked and depraved generation, in which you shine like the stars in the universe as you hold out the word of life—in order that I may boast on the day of Christ that I did not labor for nothing.

The Apostle Paul said our salvation is a process we are to "work out" in our lives with much "fear and trembling." Most people come to their salvation through this process of constantly seeking and searching for it, but some are born again in a more explosive manner, and with great emotional impact. Some people experience a great emotional outpouring when they are saved, while others are more restrained. This difference is due to their personalities and makeup, and in no way represents their "level" of spirituality.

A common denominator found in all who are truly saved, is their knowing they are no longer the person they used to be. They know their entire makeup has been changed, and they see things in a different light. This is the best way I can describe what being regenerated is like, and every believer I have met knows what I mean by being "different" than they used to be. God's Word tells us more about this in I Corinthians 15:45–52:

> If there is a natural body, there is also a spiritual body. So it is written: The first man Adam became a living being, the last Adam, a life-giving spirit. The spiritual did not come first, but the natural, and after that the spiritual. The first man was of the dust of the earth, the second man from heaven. As was the earthly man,

> so are those who are of the earth; as is the man from heaven, so also are those who are of heaven. And just as we have borne the likeness of the earthly man, so shall we bear the likeness of the man from heaven. I declare to you, brothers, that flesh and blood cannot inherit the kingdom of God, nor does the perishable inherit the imperishable. Listen, I tell you a mystery: We will not all sleep, but we will all be changed—in a flash, in the twinkling of an eye, at the last trumpet.

The Apostle Paul told us we will not inherit the kingdom of God unless we are changed spiritually. This truth is taught throughout the Scriptures, and it is one of the most important doctrinal truths. If we stay in the natural state we were physically born into, we will never reach a heavenly existence with God. Jesus and Paul both taught this same message in many different passages of Scripture. We must be born again to reach God's kingdom; there is no other way.

The Bible teaches us that this experience of being born again comes from our belief in Jesus Christ as our Savior. This fact is pointed out in many passages, such as in John 14:6–7; "Jesus answered, 'I am the way and the truth and the life. No one comes to the Father except through me. If you really knew me, you would know my Father as well. From now on, you do know him and have seen him.' " This passage clearly states that Jesus declared Himself to be the only way to reach the Father in Heaven. Another passage stating this fact is found in Acts 4:11–12; "He is the stone you builders rejected, which has become the capstone. Salvation is found in no one else, for there is no other name under heaven given to men by which we must be saved."

The sovereign deity of our Lord Jesus is declared

throughout the Scriptures, and His position as the sole means for us to receive salvation is proclaimed as well. To deny either of these doctrines is to ignore what is plainly revealed to us in God's Word. So now we have clearly seen that in order to become a Christian we must be spiritually born again, and we have also learned that Jesus Christ is the only one who can accomplish this for us. Now that we have learned these truths, we will look at what it takes for us to gain this gift of eternal life through God's only Son.

However, before moving on, I want to share a passage which should help you to understand the importance of praying for the Holy Spirit's help when reading from Scripture. It is so important to ask for His help, because truth is revealed through Him. We can read the Scriptures for ourselves, but it is the Holy Spirit who reveals the meaning of what is written. This is stated in 1 Corinthians 2:6–14:

> We do, however, speak a message of wisdom among the mature, but not the wisdom of this age or of the rulers of this age, who are coming to nothing. No, we speak of God's secret wisdom, a wisdom that has been hidden and that God destined for our glory before time began. None of the rulers of this age understood it, for if they had, they would not have crucified the Lord of glory. However, as it is written: "No eye has seen, no ear has heard, no mind has conceived what God has prepared for those who love him"—but God revealed it to us by his Spirit.
>
> The Spirit searches all things, even the deep things of God. For who among men knows the thoughts of a man except the man's spirit within him? In the same way

> no one knows the thoughts of God except the Spirit of God. We have not received the spirit of the world but the Spirit who is from God, that we may understand what God has freely given us. This is what we speak, not in words taught us by human wisdom but in words taught by the Spirit, expressing spiritual truths in spiritual words. The man without the Spirit does not accept the things that come from the Spirit of God, for they are foolishness to him, and he cannot understand them, because they are spiritually discerned.

That passage states how our understanding of God's Word comes from the Holy Spirit's guidance. This makes perfect sense, because it was the same Spirit who inspired the authors to write what is in our Bible. We need to pray for His help in understanding what we read and hear from the Bible, so we can have a better grasp of what God is teaching us in His Word.

So, now let's look at the first thing which happens in order for us to become a Christian. Scripture teaches that the first thing to happen is our being called by God. It is God who initiates the process of our regeneration. This is found in Romans 8:28–29:

> And we know that in all things God works for the good of those who love him, who have been called according to his purpose. For those God foreknew he also predestined to be conformed to the likeness of his Son, that he might be the firstborn among many brothers.

That passage from Romans states how God works for the good of those who have been called by Him according to His purpose. A similar passage can be found in 2 Timothy 1:8–10:

> So do not be ashamed to testify about our Lord, or ashamed of me his prisoner. But join with me in suffering for the gospel, by the power of God, who has saved us and called us to a holy life—not because of anything we have done but because of his own purpose and grace. This grace was given to us in Christ Jesus before the beginning of time, but it has now been revealed through the appearing of our Savior, Christ Jesus, who has destroyed death and has brought life and immortality to light through the gospel.

God is the one who calls and saves us, and not because of anything we have done to deserve it. It is God's doing, not ours. We cannot initiate our regeneration, we can only pray and ask God to do it for us. We must reach a point where we know we are helpless, and ask God to save us. We must say, "Lord Jesus, please come into our heart." We need to ask God to save us, by hoping and praying for Him to do so.

One more passage we can look at is John 6:44; "No one can come to me unless the Father who sent me draws him, and I will raise him up at the last day." There is no one who will be saved unless the Father first draws them, and then Jesus Christ will raise them up. Jesus said that only after God draws us to Him, can we be saved. So we need to understand that God draws us towards His Son in order for us to begin a relationship with Him. The thing so many miss is the fact that it is God who will make us hunger and thirst after this relationship. I have talked with many believers about their personal condition of the heart, and many have said they craved this relationship in a way they never had before, once they knew God was drawing them towards His Son. Although they had spent much time in reading the Scriptures, attending church services, prayer, and other religious activities, they knew something different had taken hold of them. They knew they were not as they used to be, and everything about God and His righteousness meant more to them than ever before.

This is something very hard for a non-believer to comprehend. Maybe you are someone like I was, and it could help you to understand if I share from my own personal experience of the difference that took place in my life when I was drawn by God. I was someone who read my Bible religiously. I attended church. I prayed. I served in a children's program. I felt I was trying to follow God. But, then there came a day when I realized I wanted to please God in a way I never had before. I couldn't get enough of His Word, and I came to see that something had changed in my heart; this change was because God had drawn me to Himself.

I no longer read the Bible because I thought I was "supposed" to read it. The same was true about my prayer life. I no longer just went through the motions whenever some bad situation came up, or when some great blessing happened in my life; I pray now because I want to talk with my Father in Heaven. I attend church services so I can grow in my faith, and because it is where I learn about what God has said to us in His Word. It was no longer because it was required in order to play on the church softball team. These are the types of changes I experienced in my own life, and other believers have expressed the same types of changes in theirs. This is the result of God's calling us to Himself; not because of some decision we made to turn over a new leaf. You can try that turning over thing, but you will find you always manage to get back to where you started.

There has been a change, and it didn't come from anything I did. It wasn't because I decided it was time to do something different, and I can't stress that point strongly enough. The reason I say that, is because I had decided to do something different so many times before, like making a New Year's resolution, but how long do you keep them? Maybe a diet or exercise resolution for a short time, but try making a resolution about changing the entire direction of your life...good luck! It's not going to happen; never has and never will! Men are too weak in our flesh, and we cannot overcome that condition with our own strength.

So I ask you, if you find yourself suddenly able to overcome obstacles you never could before, or if you desire to know and please God in ways you never did before; do you believe it was you who was responsible for this sudden change in your life? It was not you who instituted this change; it was God! God has performed a supernatural work in your body, and given you a new heart. He has removed the heart of stone that was there, and replaced it with one of flesh that desires to know Him. It is only after God has performed this changing of your heart when you will find yourself hungering and thirsting after His righteousness. This change is the next step in our salvation; it is the supernatural regeneration of our heart as we are born again.

This experience of being born again is one of the most difficult for a non-believer to understand. It is also very difficult for those who profess to be Christians, and yet say they are not the born again type. This is a self-condemning position, because there is no other type of believer defined in Scriptures. As we read earlier in the book of John, Jesus made it perfectly clear that unless you are born again, you will not see God's kingdom.

I noticed during the election cycle in 2006, there were many references made by political candidates about their Christian heritage and backgrounds. I also heard candidates during interviews on the news saying they were not the born again type of Christian. That is because this world has successfully labeled those who profess to be born again Christians as being bigoted, exclusive, and right-wing radical individuals. If you can be called a "liberal" Christian, you can fit more easily into the accepted mold of a religious person in politics. If you can separate your religious life from your political life, then you are going to fit better into the scheme of acceptance necessary to succeed in politics. The problem with this position is that there is nothing in this world which carries the significance equal to your spiritual relationship with God.

We must be born again and receive a regenerated heart, in order to see the kingdom of God. Another passage telling us this is found in 2 Corinthians 5:17–18; "Therefore, if anyone is in Christ, he is a new creation; the old has gone, the new has come! All this is from God, who reconciled us to himself through Christ and gave us the ministry of reconciliation." This passage states once again how anyone who is a Christian is a new creation. Your old self is gone, and a new self has been given to you as a gift from God. We must not overlook that it is God who makes all of this happen for us. It is God who regenerates our stony hearts, and gives us one of flesh so we can hunger and thirst after His righteousness. Another passage proclaiming this fact is found in Ephesians 2:8–10; "For it is by grace you have been saved, through faith—and this not from yourselves, it is the gift of God—not by works, so that no one can boast. For we are God's workmanship, created in Christ Jesus to do good works, which God prepared in advance for us to do."

Taking these two passages together, we find the truth about our salvation; it is a gift from God. It is not due to anything which we have done. We are born again by the grace of God, through our faith in His Son. It is given to us as a gift; not as something we have earned. There are no works or actions we can do to receive this gift, or we would have a reason to boast. That passage in Ephesians makes it clear that we are God's workmanship, and not our own. We will perform acts of good works and service, but we will do them because we are saved, not in order to be saved.

God performs the regeneration of our hearts as His own free gift of grace. This is found once again in 1 Peter 1:3–4; "Praise be to the God and Father of our Lord Jesus Christ! In his great mercy he has given us new birth into a living hope through the resurrection of Jesus Christ from the dead, and into an inheritance that can never perish, spoil or fade—kept in Heaven for you." Once again, we are told this gift comes from God's great mercy, and this gift is a new birth. We are born again into the living hope which comes from the resurrection of Jesus Christ, into an inheritance that will never perish. The theme running throughout all of these passages is the same: God bestows this gift of regeneration upon us out of His own grace, and nothing we do can earn it in any way.

There is a difficulty which comes up when someone believes they are in control of their salvation. They can convince themselves there is no urgency in the timing of this born again experience. I know this from personal experience, because I found myself thinking just that way when I was a teenager. I believed I could just wait and tell God yes when I was an old man, so I didn't believe I needed to do it any time soon. I didn't want to give up the things of this world while I was young. I wanted to enjoy the sinful activities bringing me pleasure. Why should I give them up, when I could just wait and tell God I was ready to be saved later on?

As stated earlier in chapter seven, this notion of just waiting for our salvation can be a very unhealthy one. One obvious danger is the possibility we may pass away at an early age, leaving us in eternal separation from God. Another bad possibility comes from the fact that as we become older and more controlled by this world, our hearts become harder and more like stone. It will become much less likely for us to seek after God as we become hardened through our willful life of sin.

This truth is found written in Hebrews 3:7–15:

> So, as the Holy Spirit says: "Today, if you hear his voice, do not harden your hearts as you did in the rebellion, during the time of testing in the desert, where your fathers tested and tried me and for forty years saw what I did. That is why I was angry with that generation, and I said, 'Their hearts are always going astray, and they have not known my ways.' So I declared an oath in my anger, 'They shall never enter my rest.'
>
> See to it brothers, that none of you has a sinful, unbelieving heart that turns away from the living God. But encourage one another daily, as long as it is called Today, so that none of you may be hardened by sin's deceitfulness. We have come to share in Christ if we hold firmly till the end the confidence we had at first. As has just been said: "Today, if you hear his voice, do not harden your hearts as you did in the rebellion."

This passage serves as a warning for us. It uses the example of the Hebrews as they wandered in the wilderness after being freed from captivity in Egypt. Because they hardened their hearts in the desert and tested God, they were not allowed to enter into the land promised to them. We are warned not to live our lives in this same manner. This lifestyle hardens our hearts through the deceitfulness of prolonged sinful activity, and it arouses God's anger, which places us into a very dangerous position.

Calling it *arrogance* is another way to describe this belief that we can determine the timing of our salvation. We need to keep in perspective who we are, and who God is. This is something we should always keep clear in our minds and hearts, to avoid even a hint of this arrogant attitude. A good place to see this illustrated is found in the book of Psalm 8:3–9:

> When I consider your heavens, the work of your fingers, the moon and the stars, which you have set in place, what is man that your are mindful of him, the son of man that you care for him? You made him a little lower than the heavenly beings and crowned him with glory and honor. You made him ruler over the works of your hands; you put everything under his feet: all flocks and herds, and the beasts of the field, the birds of the air and the fish of the sea, all that swim the paths of the seas. O lord, our Lord, how majestic is your name in all the earth!

The psalmist has done a wonderful job of describing how we should feel when we consider ourselves against the backdrop of God's creation. It is hard around all of our well-lit areas to find a place where we can gaze into the sky and see the immensity of the stars in the universe, but if you can get away to a place where you can; stand still and look at them. If you do, you will understand what the psalmist meant when he gazed at them and asked himself, "What is man, that God should consider him at all?" If you see even a small part of the infinite beauty surrounding us, you will see why the psalmist recognized his own insignificance in the grand scheme of this universe God has created. He understood that man is not the ultimate power in this universe; he is not even noteworthy.

Understanding this fact places us all in a better position. It helps us to change the way we see our God. It helps us to see what a tremendous gift God offered us in sending His only Son as a living sacrifice for us. As insignificant as we are, God still valued our souls, and considered them worth saving. We need to fall on our knees and thank Him for His grace and mercy! God offered His gift of salvation to us even though we were unworthy, as found in Romans 5:8; "But God demonstrated His own love for us in this: While we were still sinners, Christ died for us."

Every one of us should spend time meditating on this. Jesus Christ came and died for us even though we were unrepentant sinners. Can we even begin to grasp the magnitude of this fact? It is impossible for man, with his limited mind, to truly see the great mercy God has shown to us. The psalmist was trying to express this when he saw his own irrelevance against the background of God's creation. If you fail to see yourself in this same manner, try doing like the psalmist did; gaze at God's creation.

When it comes to our salvation, we need to look at it as an ongoing affair, as the Apostle Paul tells us in Philippians 2:12; "Therefore, my dear friends, as you have always obeyed—not only in my presence, but now much more in my absence—

continue to work out your salvation with fear and trembling." I could never offer a better piece of advice than what Paul stated in that passage. No matter how comfortable you may be with your own understanding of where you are spiritually, never stop trying to attain a higher level of salvation! It doesn't matter if you were saved by offering a sinner's prayer during an evangelical service, or if it came while reading a Bible tract, or if it came when a friend shared Scripture; whatever method led you to your profession of faith is irrelevant in and of itself. The bottom line is, you were seeking and searching for God's forgiveness at that time, and you should never stop.

If you cannot see a true change in your life after making this profession, you need to double your efforts at finding God. Is it possible you were not truly sincere in your desire to become a Christian, and therefore God has not regenerated your heart? If you never see any evidence of your faith, even though you try to be a better person, maybe you haven't really trusted in God yet.

If any of these conditions describe you, then you need to ask God to save you once more. Follow the instructions Paul gave, and continue working on your salvation with fear and trembling. Never stop acknowledging before God how unworthy you are, and your inability to do anything about it. Let Him know you want to be saved, and ask Him to grant you His undeserved mercy. When He does, there will come a point in your life when you will realize you are a new creature. You will begin to see the evidence which was lacking before, and you will know you have been born again. Then you will thank God for what He has done for you, in a way you have never felt before.

When you have been brought to your salvation, you will then be at the point the Scriptures call justification. This is when we know our sins have been forgiven through the shed blood of Jesus on the Cross. We are justified by the atonement of our sins through His sacrifice. There was nothing we could have done for our sins to justify ourselves, but God presented the perfect sacrifice for us in the embodiment of His only Son on the Cross.

We can read about this in Romans 3:21–28:

> But now a righteousness from God, apart from law, has been made known, to which the Law and the Prophets testify. This righteousness from God comes through faith in Jesus Christ to all who believe. There is no difference, for all have sinned and fall short of the glory of God, and are justified freely by his grace through the redemption that came by Christ Jesus. God presented him as a sacrifice of atonement, through faith in his blood. He did this to demonstrate his justice, because in his forbearance he had left the sins committed beforehand unpunished—he did it to demonstrate his justice at the present time, so as to be just and the one who justifies those who have faith in Jesus.
>
> Where, then, is boasting? It is excluded. On what principle? On that of observing the law? No, but on that of faith. For we maintain that a man is justified by faith apart from observing the law.

So we are justified through our faith in Jesus' sacrificial death on the Cross, and not by observing the law or anything else we do or believe in can get us there. It is completely by God's grace, and only after seeking His forgiveness, that we find our justification through believing in His Son's shed blood at Calvary.

Another passage about our justification can be found in Romans 5:8–11:

> But God demonstrates his own love for us in this: While we were still sinners, Christ died for us. Since we have now been justified by his blood, how much more shall we be saved from God's wrath through him! For if, when we were God's enemies, we were reconciled to him through the death of his Son, how much more, having been reconciled, shall we be saved through his life! Not only is this so, but we also rejoice in God through our Lord Jesus Christ, through whom we have now received reconciliation.

We should live our life as this passage proclaims for us! Rejoice, because God has saved you through His Son's death on the Cross, and your sins can be forgiven! While we were yet sinners and enemies of God, we were saved! Justified by His shed blood and the grace of God! Such is the standing of every born again believer, and we need to let the whole world know the good news; we all can be forgiven! This is our calling: to let the world know the good news of salvation. We must let others know we have been saved, and how we were. We must let them know it was through God's grace and our faith in His Son, that we have become born again, and it is a gift from God. Let them know God has called us to Himself, and given us a new heart, for a new life.

From the point of regeneration on, we are new creations. We are justified by Jesus' blood; not by our faith in His blood, but by His blood itself. Our faith comes from the new heart God has given to us. My heartfelt prayer is for all to reach the point of knowing their salvation. The sooner you ask God to forgive you, the better.

It is very good for us when we can see ourselves for the unworthy subjects we really are. Then we can finally turn to God and cry out for Him to help us, because we know we cannot help ourselves. We need to approach God in a spirit of complete humbleness and brokenness. He will hear you, because that is the way Scripture teaches us to seek Him.

Once we have received this gift of salvation, it is forever and always. By that I refer to once we have truly been saved, and not merely having falsely convinced ourselves we have been. There are many whom we are told will convince themselves in this way, but they will be false converts. We read about this in Matthew 7:21–23:

> Not everyone who says to me Lord, Lord, will enter the kingdom of heaven, but only he who does the will of my Father who is in heaven. Many will say to me on that day, Lord, Lord, did we not prophesy in your name, and in your name drive out demons and perform many miracles? Then I will tell them plainly, I never knew you. Away from me, you evildoers.

In this passage, Jesus told us there will not be only a few who will mistakenly believe they have been saved, but many. Only those who do the Will of His Father will see Heaven, and the only way we can do God's will is to be regenerated. It is the motivation behind what we do which matters the most to God, not the actual works themselves. The only way our works will please God, is if we are living and performing them according to His will. Then we will be doing them to please Him, and because we want to please Him. There will be no selfish motivation behind them, including the purpose of trying to earn our salvation. Though the acts mentioned in that passage would seem to be pleasing to God, those who performed them were called evildoers. They were called this because of the states of their hearts, and that is why Jesus tells them He never knew them.

If your heart is still one of stone, it is the same one with which you were physically born. That means you are in the same condition as the men from that passage: unknown to Jesus. It is only after you are born again and given a new heart that you become a child of God, and Jesus becomes your brother. Your works will not help you reach God, but once you have been born again, your works will shine forth as evidence of your faith. We find this in James 2:18–19; "But someone will say, You have faith; I have deeds. Show me your faith without deeds, and I will show you my faith by what I do. You believe that there is one God. Good! Even the demons believe that—and shudder."

In that passage, we are shown that although our works will not lead us into salvation, they can serve us as one of the proofs of our having been saved. A good way to understand this is to think of the different works you have done in God's service, and how you felt while doing them. If you know the only reason you performed them was for the good of God's kingdom, you are doing them for the right reason. If you realize that partly you do them because you think it will help you gain some type of honor from other men or respect from God; you are doing them for the wrong reasons. Search your own heart, and determine which reasons are behind your acts of service; they can serve as evidence of your faith, or your lack of it.

Performing acts of faithful service for God's kingdom, and

striving to become more Christ-like, are both signs you are undergoing the process the Bible calls sanctification. This is the process of separating yourself from the world, and dedicating yourself unto God. It is a process of developing into the image of Christ, which every believer should undergo while here on earth. The process of sanctification is another proof of our belonging to God, and serves as further evidence of our faith. It is ongoing and continues throughout the rest of our lives on earth. It is what many refer to as our "Christian walk" or our "maturity level" as believers.

We can find references for this process of sanctification in many places from God's Word. One of them is found in 1 Corinthians 6:9–11:

> Do you not know that the wicked will not inherit the kingdom of God? Do not be deceived: Neither the sexually immoral nor idolaters nor adulterers nor male prostitutes nor homosexual offenders nor thieves nor the greedy nor drunkards nor slanderers nor swindlers will inherit the kingdom of God. And that is what some of you were. But you were washed, you were sanctified, you were justified in the name of the Lord Jesus Christ and by the Spirit of our God.

As we see from this passage, the Apostle Paul warned us not to falsely believe we can be children of God, and still continue in the types of behaviors he mentions in this passage. He mentions activities like slandering and swindling, greed and drunkenness; right alongside sexual immoralities such as adultery and homosexuality. In today's society, many who profess to be Christian try to elevate sexual sins to a higher level of wrongdoing than other sinful activities, especially when it comes to homosexual activity. The Apostle Paul did no such thing. He told us they were all unacceptable in the life of a believer.

Paul also stated these were behaviors which we were guilty of before our salvation, but should not be any longer. Growing beyond constantly falling into these sinful activities comes from our process of sanctification. Where you are in your growth process will determine how well you are able to overcome these temptations. Sanctification is a never-ending process. You need to realize you will never gain perfection while living on this planet. Only after we see Christ in Heaven, will we be made wholly perfect into His image. The key is to be able to see our progress while we are still here on earth, and let this progress serve as evidence of our faith being sincere and true.

This sanctification is worked in us with the help of the Holy Spirit, who enters into our hearts at the time of our being saved. Through our cooperating with Him as He guides us along our path towards spiritual maturity, we will become more and more like Christ. The better we are at listening to and following His directions, the farther we will travel in our Christian walk. In the same respect, if we fail to pay attention to His instructions, we will stumble. Remember, none of us will ever be perfect. Jesus Christ was and is the only one who will ever be able to accomplish the state of perfection while living here on earth. With the Holy Spirit's help, we should reach a point in our walk where the unsaved people we meet should be able to see a light in us that doesn't exist in them. This light will serve as a beacon for them, and they will want to find out where it comes from; that is when our opportunities to witness for Christ will come. There should be a distinct difference between the walk of a believer, and the walk of someone who is still lost in their sins. As we mature in our walk and travel farther in our faith, this distinct difference will become even greater.

Another passage dealing with sanctification can be found in 1 Thessalonians 4:1–8:

> Finally, brothers, we instructed you how to live in order to please God, as in fact you are living. Now we ask you and urge you in the Lord Jesus to do this more and more. For you know what instructions we gave you by the authority of the Lord Jesus.
>
> It is God's will that you should be sanctified: that you should avoid sexual immorality; that each of you should learn to control his own body in a way that is holy and honorable, not in passionate lust like the heathen, who do not know God; and that in this matter no one should wrong his brother or take advantage of him. The Lord will punish men for all such sins, as we have already told you and warned you. For God did not call us to be impure, but to live a holy life. Therefore, he who rejects this instruction does not reject man but God, who gives you his Holy Spirit.

In this passage, we find God calling on us to live a pure life—one that is holy. He has given us instructions about how we are supposed to live as Christians. Jesus gave us a description of the life a believer should live in His Sermon on the Mount, which can be found in the fifth, sixth, and seventh chapters of the book of Matthew. I urge you to read His message from that sermon as often as you can, and burn what is written there onto your heart. When you do, it will be there for you to use whenever you need help in your walk. We see again in this passage from 1 Thessalonians, that there should be a difference between the believer and the unbeliever (heathen). We are also warned of our Lord's promise to punish men who do not live a life which is pure or holy. Remember, the believer will not achieve perfection while here on earth, but with the Spirit's help, he or she should be constantly improving and growing in his or her walk of faith.

We should notice how, in this passage, the Apostle Paul stresses for us to strive to live this life more and more, and that it should be a continuing process as we grow. What a good definition of the sanctification process: becoming more and more Christ-like as we travel along in our Christian life. If you want to travel as far as possible down this path, you need to learn how to hear the Spirit's voice as He tries to guide you. It is difficult to explain this ability to someone who hasn't been born again, because the first contact we have with Him is when we become a Christian. He then places the desire on our heart to know God, and to begin our relationship with Him. Once the Holy Spirit has entered your heart, He then will be with you there for the rest of your life.

After you have been born again, the Spirit will begin speaking to you. He does this through suggesting paths we should follow to begin moving in our Christian walk. When you begin listening to, and following His guidance, you will feel a peace that lets you know you are in God's will. This peace is described in Philippians 4:4–7:

> Rejoice in the Lord always. I will say it again: Rejoice! Let your gentleness be evident to all. The Lord is near. Do not be anxious about anything, but in everything,

> by prayer and petition, with thanksgiving, present your requests to God. And the peace of God, which transcends all understanding, will guard your hearts and your minds in Christ Jesus.

This peace escapes the understanding of sinful man, because he is still struggling with life's issues to the point of much anxiety. Although the unrepentant man experiences happiness from the things which please him in his life, he still suffers much more than the believer does when things happen, bringing stress and pain into his life. The believer experiences a joy that can rise above the trials of life. It doesn't mean they don't still feel pain and disappointment over life's troubles, but it does mean they can rise above them. This helps to reflect the joy coming from the knowledge of having God in charge, and in control, of everything touching us in this life.

Some people call the Spirit's guidance their conscience, and that is a pretty good way of describing Him. When you are following God's will for your life, the Holy Spirit will grant you His peace, and you will feel the sensation which comes from knowing you are doing what is right. If the opposite is true, and you find yourself going against or refusing to follow God's will, the Holy Spirit will convict you for your unacceptable behavior. It can be hard sometimes to recognize the difference between the Holy Spirit's convicting of your behavior, and the devil's condemnation of it. The devil will try to make you feel like a complete failure for your mistakes along your walk, and he will try to push you into activities which will add to your downfall. The Holy Spirit, on the other hand, will try to encourage you to correct your errant behavior by making you recognize it as such. He doesn't condemn you for your failings, the devil does. The Holy Spirit doesn't try to push you into activities at all; He simply tries to lead you into ones He knows God desires for your life. When you feel coerced into doing something you didn't really want to, that could very well be the pushing of the devil which I have described. The Holy Spirit will not try to control your behavior in the same type of manner as the devil. He chooses to suggest proper behavior for us, and waits for us to exercise our own free will in deciding for ourselves what direction we will take.

A good passage from Scripture on the Holy Spirit's presence is found in John 14:25–26; "All this I have spoken while still with you. But the Counselor, the Holy Spirit, whom the Father will send in my name, will teach you all things and will remind you of everything I have said to you." Now there is a great explanation of who the Holy Spirit is, and what He does. He is our Counselor. He is sent by God to teach us everything we will ever need to know about God's Word. He helps us to understand what Jesus meant by the things He said while He was here on earth, and what God meant in the things He put down for us in the Scriptures. He was sent for our benefit, because we need His insight in order to understand what God's will is for our lives, and what the meaning in His Word is, too. In your beginning as a believer, you will probably struggle some with trying to hear the Holy Spirit's voice. As you start to mature, you should start to hear Him more easily.

This world has a way of drowning out the Spirit's voice, with the cares and concerns it brings into our lives. Even so, once we begin to earnestly try to hear Him, we find we are able to. It is just like any other part of your Christian faith; never stop trying to improve from where you are to where you want to be. The Counselor was sent to help us, and He will never leave you once you have been born again. That is a promise from God.

To look at another passage on the Holy Spirit's mission, we can turn to 1 Peter 1:1–2:

> Peter, an apostle of Jesus Christ, to God's elect, strangers in the world, scattered throughout Pontus, Galatia, Cappadocia, Asia and Bithynia, who have been chosen according to the foreknowledge of God the Father, through the sanctifying work of the Spirit, for obedience to Jesus Christ and sprinkling by his blood.

When we look at this passage closely, we notice how believers are called strangers in this world. This is because once you have been born again, you are no longer a follower of the ruler of this world: satan. You have been chosen by God to be separate from the world, and you will be sanctified by the working of the Spirit. We also see here that the purpose of the Holy Spirit's working in us is to help us to become obedient to the teachings of Jesus Christ. These teachings are so important for us as believers, and once again I must urge you to read His Sermon on the Mount, which is found in the book of Matthew, chapters 5, 6, and 7. Remember to pray for help from the Holy Spirit, so you can understand what is written there. It's His purpose and pleasure to do for us, so we will know the good Will of our Father in Heaven; so let Him do His work in you.

That is the description of the sanctification process which all believers become a part of, from the instant they are regenerated by God. They will continue in this process, until they are finally made perfect in Heaven. We are meant to grow in our faith through this process, and it is the Holy Spirit's job to help us see where we should be going. Our maturity as believers does not depend upon our age as humans (many younger people do a better job of following the Holy Spirit's guidance than do some of us older ones). Our progress is based more on our willingness to "die to self" and surrender all to God's will, than it is upon our physical age. The benefits of being more in touch with the Holy Spirit are unlimited, and worth striving for. Peace and joy becomes possible for us, no matter how difficult the situations may be which we encounter. That is a benefit everyone should recognize as being worth reaching out for!

Our sanctification process will continue until we are finally made perfect, when we see our Lord Jesus in Heaven. Then, we will be glorified through our faith in His shed blood. This final stage of our Christian walk is found in Romans 8:28–30:

> And we know that in all things God works for the good of those who love him, who have been called according to his purpose. For those God foreknew he also predestined to be conformed to the likeness of his Son, that he might be the firstborn among many brothers. And those he predestined, he also called; those he called, he also justified; those he justified, he also glorified.

This glorification is our final and perfect condition as Christian followers of our Lord Jesus Christ. It is the condition we will be in for the rest of eternity with Him and our Father who saved us through His grace and mercy. We can read of this in 1 Peter 5:1–5:

> To the elders among you, I appeal as a fellow elder,

> a witness of Christ's sufferings and one who also will share in the glory to be revealed: Be shepherds of God's flock that is under your care, serving as overseers—not because you must, but because you are willing, as God wants you to be; not greedy for money, but eager to serve; not lording it over those entrusted to you, but being examples to the flock. And when the Chief Shepherd appears, you will receive the crown of glory that will never fade away.

That is our final objective: to "receive the crown of glory that will never fade away." It is what every Christian looks forward to, and what every non-believer should be trying to find. Pray that you may see this crown a little more clearly as you are searching and seeking God's forgiveness. I hope you can see what must take place in your heart to become a Christian, and what should happen in your life after you have become one. There are so many different signals being sent by those who profess to be Christians, and I pray what I have tried to share will help you as you try to understand what Christianity is all about. I hope I have helped to ignite a desire in you to ask God for His gift of eternal life through His Son, which will never be extinguished until is it fulfilled. If you have not already been blessed with God's forgiveness, I pray you will be blessed by God soon as a new member of His family of born again believers.

Chapter Eleven

I'm a Believer...Or Am I? Take the Test

In this chapter we are going to look at what is one of the most inner reflecting questions we can ask ourselves: am I helping or hurting the cause of Christianity? I have found the best approach for answering this all important question is to first ask yourself whether or not you are convinced of your own faith being genuine. Next, we should look at what evidence from our life has led us to our understanding of our own belief. You can make this determination by looking at the conditions which exist in your daily walk, and deciding whether they represent living in a godly manner, or a worldly one. By doing this, you are fulfilling what the Scriptures say to do in Philippians 2:12; "Therefore, my dear friends, as you have always obeyed—not only in my presence, but now much more in my absence—continue to work out your salvation with fear and trembling." After we have looked into this, we will then look at how we, as believers, can best be used to witness to the unsaved through our walk and our words.

The true answer to whether or not our faith is genuine is what will determine where our souls spend the rest of eternity—either in Heaven with our Father or in Hell through separation from Him. There is no condition on earth carrying as much significance as does this one for each and every one of us. When you truly understand this fact, you will also understand how disastrous it could be not to evaluate your faith's authenticity, so consider your own life with complete honesty.

So, first let's look at trying to determine whether or not our faith is truly genuine, or simply imagined and hoped for. How can we determine whether we are a truly born-again believer, versus just being a false one? I am going to offer some observations which I have made from my own life experience, as well as from others who have shared with me on this subject, and hopefully they will help you as you reflect on them in your own life. I urge you to prayerfully consider them, and apply them with an open mind and heart.

One observation which I have made while talking with fellow believers is how many of those who claim their place in God's family the loudest, and who are the most completely assured of their salvation tend to be the ones who show the least signs of being truly repentant for their sinful lifestyle. On the other hand, many of the ones who seem to feel they are never quite repentant enough to qualify as believers are the ones who display true repentance in their walk. This type of observation can maybe be more easily made by an outside observer than it can be for us to make it about ourselves. So as you start this process of your inner reflection, I cannot stress too strongly how you must be completely honest with yourself. What you find may hurt you deeply, but it could also be what saves you from eternal separation from God! So, be completely honest. Try to see yourself as if you were standing outside of your own body, introducing yourself to yourself. This may sound different from anything you have heard before, but try it; it works.

So there you are, meeting yourself for perhaps the first time. How do you feel? Is there a little too much of a sense of self-assurance about your place in God's kingdom? I don't mean just a firm belief in the promises of salvation as they are taught in Scripture, but rather a sense of somehow having reached a point in your life when you actually believe that you now "deserve" to get into Heaven. We should never come to believe in quite that way, because we should realize the truth of our continuing to commit additional sins as we travel our paths in life. We need to remember to continually confess them to God, and to ask for His forgiveness. God did not tell us that once we are born-again, we will stop sinning; however, He did tell us how to avoid sinning, and this is found in James 4:7; "Submit yourselves, then, to God. Resist the devil, and he will flee from you."

Those who show the most remorse for their sins tend to be the ones who still fear for their salvation, which is exactly what the Apostle Paul meant in Philippians 2:12; "Therefore, my dear friends, as you have always obeyed—not only in my presence, but now much more in my absence—continue to work out your salvation with fear and trembling." These people tend to still think of themselves as "bad" people, and don't see themselves as being "righteous" in God's eyes. That's because it is only through the covering of Christ's blood when our sinful nature is removed from the sight of God (not because we think we are repentant enough).

So this is my first challenge for you to consider: do you

believe in even some small way that you are basically a good person? Do you believe you are righteous enough to deserve getting into Heaven? I have heard people who have made these types of comments, such as, "I have a good heart," or "I think I'm a good person." If this is how you see yourself, then I call on you to do a re-examination of what makes you believe these comments about yourself. I am very familiar with this particular view because it was one I held for many years in regards to myself. So I urge you to take the time to look honestly at how you really feel about yourself, and your reasons for believing as you do.

This world has a way of reinforcing these beliefs in our own worthiness, and we need to see how this is just another trick from the enemy's camp to keep us from seeing ourselves as we truly are. Maybe you are blessed with the type of personality which tends to please those you come to meet, or at least not to irritate them. Maybe you have the ability to refrain from using vulgar and coarse language. Maybe you don't suffer from fits of extreme anger, which can result in displays of uncontrolled temper. Maybe you are the type who people say is mild-mannered, and wouldn't hurt a fly. I'm sure you have at least known people who are like that, and maybe you are one of them.

It is nice when your personality enables you to exhibit these types of qualities others around you can grow to admire, but there is also a danger coming from them; be careful not to see yourself as already being Christ-like. This condition brings a serious danger with it, because you can find yourself believing in your own "righteousness" to the point of not being able to see your own need to be saved just like all others who fall short; you may not see your own shortfall.

Please do not dismiss this thought as meaningless if you

are someone with this type of personality. I know it is my own personality type, and I know I was guilty of this very way of believing in myself for many years. Your version may be a little different in some way, but the concept rings true in every case. When someone falls victim to this wrong belief, it can be very difficult for them to realize it. It is because people like this can easily see themselves as morally and socially superior to those around them, and therefore can come to see themselves as already being good enough to reach Heaven. I'm not saying everyone who has this type of personality will be guilty of this mistake, but I will say I wasn't the only one.

One thing I have found in those who try this method of inner reflection is that when they have great difficulty in performing a serious examination on a particular area of their life, it tends to be because they are not quite where they should be as a believer. This condition may show itself for you as you perform these reflections, so please keep this in mind as a litmus test as you look at yourself. The more resistant you find your heart towards your soul-searching; the more likely your heart is not as it should be in your relationship with God. This is a good point to keep in mind while trying to see the true condition of our hearts, and whether they have been made new or not.

As we look at different areas of our lives in the attempt to determine our true position in the Christian faith, it can cause us to have a healthy form of doubt. This type of doubt is not something which will keep you from reaching Heaven; but disbelief is. To doubt something is merely to question its authenticity, or to be uncertain about your position in regards to a particular belief or opinion. Doubt is a just a form of indecisiveness, but if it becomes accepted as your true position, it can become unbelief.

We find a good example of this state of doubt in John 20:24–29:

> Now Thomas (called Didymus), one of the Twelve, was not with the disciples when Jesus came. So the other disciples told him, "We have seen the Lord!"
>
> But he said to them, "Unless I see the nail marks in his hands and put my finger into his side, I will not believe it."
>
> A week later his disciples were in the house again, and Thomas was with them. Though the doors were locked, Jesus came and stood among them and said, "Peace be with you!" Then he said to Thomas, "Put your finger here; see my hands. Reach out your hand and put it into my side. Stop doubting and believe."
>
> Thomas said to him, "My Lord and my God!"
>
> Then Jesus told him, "Because you have seen me, you have believed; blessed are those who have not seen and yet have believed."

This passage created the nickname "doubting Thomas" which has lasted throughout the centuries. I am so happy our Lord used this example of His disciple, because it serves such a useful purpose for those of us who have the same, doubtful weakness as Thomas. Thomas was obviously a doubting person, because the other disciples were unable to convince him even though they testified in unison about the Lord's return. But, Thomas did not just say they were all crazy fools to believe as they claimed; that would have been unbelief instead of doubt. Thomas decided he needed proof to conquer his doubt, and he settled on a course of action which would satisfy his need for this proof. He knew in order to believe, he would need some form of physical evidence to satisfy his doubts.

This need to have proof before you can believe is not something we should call the end of the world; it certainly wasn't the end for Thomas. However, our Lord did say those who are able to believe without physical proof—such as through seeing and touching Him—are blessed. Thomas' personal makeup made it necessary for him to have something more than just faith to believe; however, pay attention to the fact that Thomas did eventually come to believe. Thomas was the type of person who we might call analytical in nature, and by this I mean he was someone who always questions everything before they can accept it as factual. I'm not saying to be this way is necessarily a bad thing; it is just a type of personality trait. The main difference between Thomas and analytical people like him and those who are able to believe without seeing and touching, come from the analytical people believing first with their minds, while the others believe first with their hearts.

In that passage from the book of John, Jesus said those who believe without seeing are blessed. It's also very comforting to know those who are like Thomas, who believe with their minds, can still be blessed through believing. So if you are someone like Thomas, and you find it difficult or nearly impossible to believe just on faith, I encourage you to be of good cheer, because you are not a lost cause! This state is another one which has always been part of my personal makeup. Many times I have driven a would-be mentor almost crazy with my endless barrage of questions about Biblical doctrines. But praise be to God! He always places the right people in front of us when we need them the most, and our analytical minds can finally relent, and accept the truth of His Word.

If you are one of us analytical types, there are some steps I would like to suggest for you to follow in your quest to believe. First off, I want you to know you are not alone. In fact, I believe the analytical people are probably the majority. Our doubt does not have to become unbelief; we just need to check out the facts. That is what Thomas did by touching the wounds in Jesus' side; he checked out the facts for himself. So we must do the same, and investigate the facts of the matter. If we fail to investigate and just let our doubt become accepted, we have fallen into unbelief, and are lost if we stay in that state.

As you begin investigating, be sure to use multiple sources of information as you prepare to make your decisions about every issue at hand. The Bible should serve as your number one source of evidence, but before it will satisfy your analytical mind, you will have had to accept it as God's infallibly written Word. This is one problem which can be very difficult for analytical types to overcome: difficulty in allowing their hearts to lead them in decisions of faith. It always helps if you pray for God to help you believe with your heart. Ask Him to help your heart to override your mind, when it refuses to accept things as being true just because God says so.

Along with your Bible, you should be listening to preaching and teaching on what is contained in God's Word. As we discussed earlier in the last chapter, don't forget to make sure you are attending a Bible-preaching church. It's also not a good idea to gather all of your information from one particular preacher or teacher. It can be very dangerous to follow one person exclusively, because you don't know if they are always sharing as they should. It is always good to hear more than one perspective, and different understandings on the same topics.

In order to deal with the doubt that remains in so many of us, we have to remember to spend time meditating on the Scripture dealing with Thomas and his doubts. It doesn't mean you aren't born again just because you still struggle with doubtful thoughts; if it did, there wouldn't be many believers at all! To some extent, I think a little doubt can even be used to our advantage when it causes us to continually search the Scriptures for the truth revealed in their pages. We just can't let our doubt turn into unbelief. We need to search for the facts, and make educated decisions about whether or not we need to be led to Christ. We must always focus our attention on Jesus Christ; He will help us to overcome our doubt.

To make an analytical decision about Jesus Christ is not as difficult a thing to do as some may make it sound. Just like any other decision you make, you simply need to look at all of the possibilities in order to decide what makes the most sense for you to believe. In looking at Jesus Christ, there are only so many possibilities to believe as to who He really was. The possible explanations for who Jesus Christ really was can be listed as: Lord, liar, lunatic, myth, or magician. These are five different categories which we can try to place Him into, and then we can look at them to decide which one makes the most sense to believe.

First, we will look at the possibility of Jesus Christ truly being our Lord and Savior; the Son of God. Regardless of what you may have heard, this is not a claim only made up by men after Jesus had left this world. Jesus made this claim Himself in numerous passages of Scripture. One of them can be found in Mark 14:60–64:

> Then the high priest stood up before them and asked Jesus, Are you not going to answer? What is this testimony that these men are bringing against you? But Jesus remained silent and gave no answer. Again the high priest asked him, Are you the Christ, the Son of the Blessed One? "I am," said Jesus, "And you will see the Son of Man sitting at the right hand of the Mighty One and coming on the clouds of heaven." The high priest tore his clothes. Why do we need any more witnesses? You have heard the blasphemy. What do you think? They all condemned him as worthy of death.

Jesus was crucified at Calvary, because the ruling religious leaders would not accept His claim to be the Christ. The question for all of us now is: will we accept Him as our Lord and Savior? Many people have fallen victim to the world's teaching of Jesus as being nothing more than a really good man, and a good teacher–maybe the best ever. Some say He was just some sort of radical political figure, who revolted against the established religious order of His day, and He was killed for doing so. Could He have really been just a very good man? Could He just have been the greatest teacher of morality the world has ever known? His "Sermon on the Mount," found in the book of Matthew, chapters 5, 6, and 7, is heralded by the world as the greatest piece of teaching on morality the world has ever known. That is what the world would have you believe about Him, and nothing more, but there is an obvious flaw to be found by the discerning mind in this description of Jesus. If He was the perfect teacher and a great man of integrity, but nothing more than that, then His claim of being the Son of God makes Him a liar.

Now let's look at the possible belief that Jesus was nothing more than a liar. Lying is something we are all familiar with, as we all find ourselves doing it from time to time. If you don't think you lie, then you are guilty of it right now. However, lying is not a trait we associate with men of great integrity. To do so is to create an oxymoron; but, it is still one of the ways this world tries to portray Jesus. So let's think about this possibility, and what this particular claim Jesus Christ made in the book of Mark cost Him. It led to His being beaten and dragged through the streets of Jerusalem, and then His Crucifixion. Knowing, from our personal experiences, how a liar thinks, do you believe a great man of integrity would tell a lie such as that, and then let them crucify Him for the telling of it? No! Jesus could not be a great man and tell such an untruth, and then allow Himself to be killed on the Cross!

Now we come to the next category He could be placed into: lunacy. This possible belief about Christ is easy to show how illogical it is. Since the world has acknowledged Him as a great teacher of morality, it denies the possibility of Him being a lunatic. If you are going to call someone great for their teaching, is it logical to also say they were not in their right mind at the same time? Yet the world thinks He deserves to be labeled "lunatic" for His so-called preposterous claims of being the Son of God.

When you think of His life and the teachings He laid down for us, can you imagine Him not being quite right in His head? It just doesn't make sense, but it is one of the possible identities the world holds out for Him, so we must either dispute or accept it. I pray for all of us with a mind for accuracy to be able to overcome this stumbling block which the world has laid, blocking our path to Christianity.

The next belief is that Jesus is nothing more than a myth

or fabrication, made up by men. The world is pushing this possibility, and actively trying to remove itself from any type of direct affirmation of Christ's existence. A great example can be found in our calendar, and how it is moving away from acknowledging two separate periods of time: before or after His existence. Documents like our Constitution used the phrase, "In the year of our Lord," which make this a more difficult thing to pull off; but, the world is fighting to make these changes with all of its might. Without a doubt, the world is going to unify on this issue of dates. We will soon be forced to change from "before Christ" to "before common era," or to whatever other label the world chooses in the place of Jesus Christ as the standard for our calendar. Some school systems have already made the transition, and are already teaching our children under one of these new methods.

But will this eliminate Christ from existence as far as the world is concerned? I should say not! The existence of Jesus Christ has been documented by more historical writings than has any other figure from history. This is the dilemma the world has been trying to overcome; but it cannot. I have had people tell me these writings are nothing but superstitions and make believe story-telling. The question is: can the world convince people of this explanation for the existence of thousands of writings about Jesus and His life? I trust not!

The last possible identity for Jesus Christ is that He was a magician. People who claim this are trying to make sense of the Scriptures which tell of the many wondrous miracles and healings He performed while here on earth. The blind were caused to see. The lame were made to walk. The deaf were made to hear. The mute were made to speak. Lepers were cleansed and made whole again. One of the most miraculous recordings of all, tells of Jesus' bringing Lazarus back from the dead, and is recorded in John 11. All of these miracles are recorded in God's Word, and serve as accounts of the supernatural power Jesus had on earth. The final miracle was the greatest of all: He rose from the grave after His crucifixion! This is the miracle which all of Christianity is based upon—Jesus' victory over death and the grave!

So another question comes up; what do you think of these miracles? Do you believe they are fabrications of man's imagination? Do you believe they were the feats of a magician? Do you believe they were truly miracles performed by the Son of God while He was here on earth, so we could more easily have the faith to believe in Him? This can be a little tougher for some to decide upon, but if you factor in that a magician would have no reason to let himself be crucified for his tricks, it is easier to overcome. You might believe a good magician could trick the Roman guards into believing he was dead on the cross when he really wasn't. However, according to historical recordings of Roman efficiency in the area of crucifixions, they simply did not make those kinds of mistakes.

When summarizing these five possible identities for Jesus Christ as being Lord, liar, lunatic, myth, or magician; which one stands out for you? I pray you have come to the right conclusion; Jesus Christ is our Lord and Savior! He is the Son of God, just as He claimed to be! I pray you are able to see this truth in your mind, and feel it with your heart! Jesus said you are blessed when your heart does believe!

Self examination is a great way to see where we really are in our spiritual life. In order to help you, I am going to place several self exams in this chapter for you to use. I pray they will help you in this important process of examining your faith. This first one starts with an imaginary situation happening in your life—your death. For many, it may prove to be a good thing it is only imagined, because you may realize you aren't ready yet to meet God on His throne. For the taking of this test, pretend you have just passed away. You find yourself standing before God on His throne, and He asks you a very simple question; "Why should I let you into my kingdom?"

Before you read on, please take some time and answer this question for yourself honestly. I don't mean in a careless, haphazard manner; I mean think it through and decide what your reply would really be. Give it the meditation such a question deserves, because there is no question which could possibly carry as much importance for you as this one does. Think it through. I am going to list the most common responses people make to this question, and maybe you will see yourself in one of them.

One of the most common answers people make is to say God should let them into Heaven because they are a lot better person than most others. They feel God should grade on some type of a curve, and if you are average or a little better than average, you should make it into Heaven. People who think this way believe the good things they have done in their lifetime should qualify them for entry into God's kingdom. Or maybe they think the bad things they have done were not terrible enough to disqualify them. It is hard to say for sure which is the case, but both are very wrong.

To dispute this answer, we can simply turn to Romans 3:23; "For all have sinned and fall short of the glory of God." This passage makes it clear for us that every single person is a sinner, and therefore falls short of the glory required for us to be with God. We are not told that if we have committed less sin than someone else, we are in a better condition than they are. Another passage which helps remove this belief in our being less guilty than others in our sinful lives, is found in James 2:10; "For whoever keeps the whole law and yet stumbles at just one point is guilty of breaking all of it." It doesn't matter how many different laws we break; breaking one is the same as breaking them all.

If you find yourself looking around at your fellow man, and thinking about how fortunate you are because you are a better man than others, try to see yourself in relation to those two passages. When you realize you are no better off than anyone else around you, you are another step closer to reaching out to God for your salvation. So if you silently told God that you should get into Heaven because you were a better person than most, I hope you have now seen this answer will not serve to gain your entry into Heaven; it may well confirm your unworthiness instead.

Another answer many people offer is that there is no reason they can give to God in their defense, because they know they have lived their lives in a sinful way, and have chosen to do so. This at least is an honest answer, but a very sad one. Are you someone who says God will deny you entry into His kingdom because you willingly chose to live a life of sin? If this is how you honestly see yourself, are you content with that answer? Does it bother you to see yourself in this way? We can read how Moses felt about living a life of sinful pleasure in the book of Hebrews, 11:25; "He chose to be mistreated along with the people of God rather than to enjoy the pleasures of sin for a short time." If you want more on this subject, you can read the whole book of Ecclesiastes. There, you will find what this very wise man wrote about the futility of man's sinful activities.

If you responded this way to this hypothetical question from God, it is a good thing you are not already standing before Him. This reminds me of one of my favorite expressions;

"Thank God it's not over, yet." This phrase applies if you answered in this way, because you still have time to seek God's forgiveness. If you are still guilty of not only living a sinful life, but also enjoying it, you are very fortunate your time on earth is not yet through.

We all need to spend time in prayer, asking God to help us reach the point of repentance for our life of sin, just as every true believer before us has done. You are no different than anyone else was before God regenerated their heart, and they were born again. When you reach that understanding, then you are on your way to finding God. You are no better or worse than any other person before you ever was or will be. Only men try to rate our lives on a scale in order to feel some man-made sense of self-righteousness.

We can read about how God views our acts of righteousness in Isaiah 64:6; "All of us have become like one who is unclean, and all our righteous acts are like filthy rags; we all shrivel up like a leaf, and like the wind our sins sweep us away." Another place we can turn to is Romans 3:10–12; "As it is written: There is no one righteous, not even one; there is no one who understands, no one who seeks God. All have turned away, they have together become worthless; there is no one who does good, not even one."

These passages should help us to see how we are no different from anyone else in regards to our personal level of self-righteousness. None of us are righteous in God's eyes. He looks at us from the heart, not from the outward appearances we show forth to others around us. So if your response was one of admitting you don't deserve to get into Heaven, and the reason for this response is because you recognize your own unworthiness, you are almost home! You have identified the truth about yourself, and your future in eternity. I pray you are not content to remain as you are, and for you to move forward to the next response many people make to this imaginary question I posed.

Some respond to the previous question about getting into Heaven, by saying that there is no reason they can think of to prove their worthiness. They also admit they are sinful people, who do things contrary to God's commands. This is very similar to the response we previously discussed. The difference between the two is that this group of people knows that they are in need. These people have seen their own weakness, and are ashamed for seeing themselves as they truly are: human. This is where they part from the previous group of people; they are not content to remain as they are. They want to be saved from their lost state, and they are seeking God's help to save them.

This group sees themselves bowing before God, admitting there is no possible reason they can offer to gain their entry into His kingdom. They realize that the only thing they can do is it admit their unworthiness, and ask for God's forgiveness and saving grace. They have realized there is nothing they can do to obtain this forgiveness on their own; it can only be received through the faith God provides to those who ask for it. This group has found the saving grace which comes from having faith in Jesus Christ, and His ability to save them. They have understood the truth as it is written in Acts 4:12; "Salvation is found in no one else, for there is no other name under heaven given to men by which we must be saved."

This is the difference between those who make these last two responses; it is all the difference it takes to reach Heaven. These people know that when they kneel before God and tell Him how sorry they are for their sinful lives, they fall short of the standard God has set for our having a relationship with

Him. They also know they can tell God they have placed their hopes and faith in His Son, and it is Jesus Christ who will speak in their defense. They have received His Son as their substitute for the punishment which God has promised must be handed out for our breaking of His commands. Thank God, Jesus has already paid our price, in full, on the Cross.

Jesus has paid the price, and His blood can cover the sins we bring with us. We can read about this in Psalm 103:11–12; "For as high as the heavens are above the earth, so great is his love for those who fear him; as far as the east is from the west, so far has he removed our transgressions from us." Another passage telling of God's forgiveness for our sins is found in Hebrews 8:12; "For I will forgive their wickedness and will remember their sins no more." These are the promises allowing us to hope to spend time with God in Heaven. It is not because of anything we have done; it is only because we have thrown ourselves at Jesus' feet and received His gift of salvation.

If this answer describes how you would respond to this hypothetical question from God, you should spend time on your knees in thankful prayer and praise to God for bringing you to this point. You have been born again into His kingdom, and His Word promises you will spend eternity with Him in Heaven. This is the best response any of us could possibly make when our time comes. We need to see how fortunate we are, because God has brought us to Himself.

With that thought, it is time to look at the most common response people make to this question; "I have no idea what I would say." At first, this response seems to be the saddest. However, when we look behind it, we can see it as another honest one. There are many people out there who really have no idea how we can get into Heaven. There are just as many who don't even know if they believe such a place exists. I have had many people tell me they don't believe in Heaven or Hell, or in the existence of God. This is very sad to hear, but it is not the end of the world for them. When I meet someone who makes this type of statement, I tell them, "Thank God it's not over yet!"

Some people make this response because they really don't know what they would say to God. Others make it because they don't believe it will ever really happen. In either case, God's Word says it will happen. This is found in Hebrews 9:27; "Just as man is destined to die once, and after that to face judgment." Before your day comes, I pray God will lead you into His Son's open arms! When it does come, it is not going to matter whether or not you believe God is real; your time for judgment is going to come regardless of what you have believed. In the end, the only thing that will matter for the rest of your eternity is whether or not you have been forgiven!

If you are unsure about what the Bible has to say about salvation, you need to find a translation which speaks to your heart. Next you need to just sit down, and read it prayerfully. You need to find a church preaching and teaching the complete Word of God, and start attending regularly. You need to get as much of God's Word into your heart as you possibly can. The bottom line is, you need a relationship with God. There is nothing as important as this in your life. So please, never stop searching for God's forgiveness.

Another self-examination we can take is found in the book of 1 John, which is sometimes called the book for doubters. Many of the verses in 1 John serve as a test we can take to affirm whether our regeneration is real. These simple tests can be worth so much to us, because they can help us understand our position in our relation to God's kingdom.

To start, let's look at 1 John 1:3–4; "We proclaim to you what we have seen and heard, so that you also may have fellowship with us. And our fellowship is with the Father and with his Son, Jesus Christ. We write this to make our joy complete." This passage describes one of the feelings a believer should have in his or her life: joy from fellowship with the Father, His Son, and with other believers. Is this a fair description of your life? Do you feel joy when you spend time in God's Word or in prayer with Him? Do you feel joy when you spend time in fellowship with others from your church family? There was a time, in my walk, when I was a specialist at getting in and out of church without having to talk to anyone, and I dodged invitations to spend time at church gatherings. If this is a behavior which you are familiar with, let me share a warning with you; examine what makes you behave in this way.

I am not implying you must stop all fellowship with non-believers, but I will say you should feel at home among your brothers and sisters in God's family. There should be a special feeling between fellow believers, and this is taught in 1 Peter 2:17; "Show proper respect to everyone: Love the brotherhood of believers, fear God, honor the King." In looking at this passage, notice how we are told to show respect to everyone; however, we are to love our fellow believers. Believers are spelled out separately, and granted extra significance. That is what I am trying to express here. If you do not feel real joy while spending time with your church family, you need to seriously contemplate what is keeping you from doing so.

Moving on, we can take a look at 1 John 1:8–9:

> If we claim to be without sin, we deceive ourselves and the truth is not in us. If we confess our sins, he is

> faithful and just and will forgive us our sins and purify us from all unrighteousness. If we claim we have not sinned, we make him out to be a liar and his word has no place in our lives.

This passage tells us how our sin will remain in our lives as believers, but when we confess our sins, God will forgive us for them. He will purify us from our unrighteousness through His process of sanctification—the growth process we are undergoing as His children. We must admit we are sinful, or we are told the truth is not really in us. If we fail to confess, it may mean we are only false believers who are just deceiving ourselves. According to this passage, anyone who says they are not a sinner is making Christ out to be a liar. If that is true for you, God's Word is not really in your heart. So the question this passage puts out for us as part of this self-examination test is this: are you aware of your sin?

As a born again believer, the Holy Spirit has entered your heart. He is there to help guide and direct you in your Christian walk. One of His duties is to make you aware of sin when it enters your life, and to help you overcome it by leading you to repentance. This can serve as another proof of your faith. Do you recognize sins when they enter your life, and do you confess them to your Father and ask for His forgiveness? As a believer, you should be highly responsive to sin whenever it creeps into your life. It should disgust you, whenever you realize you have fallen into it. Sin is something an unbeliever may be aware of, but they are not going to be as sensitive to it as one of God's children should be. So, the question this passage serves up for the believer is: are you thoroughly disgusted by the presence of sin in your life? If you do not feel you are, I urge you to meditate on why you are not.

Taking this theme of sin a step further, we can move on to 1 John 2:3–6:

> We know that we have come to know him if we obey his commands. The man who says, "I know him," but does not do what he commands is a liar, and the truth is not in him. But if anyone obeys his word, God's love is truly made complete in him. This is how we know we are in him: Whoever claims to live in him must walk as Jesus did.

When you look at this passage, there is much to consider. The main point is that true believers should strive to obey God's commands. We should be trying our best to be Christ-like. By that, I mean we should no longer live a life of constant sinning. We know there is no one who will be able to keep all of God's commands, but we will be striving to do our best at all times. We need to see that anyone who claims to know Christ, but fails to try to keep His commands is a liar. Pleasing God and following Jesus Christ's example of how to live our lives as believers should be the driving force in your life. If it's not, ask yourself why.

The next step in this self-exam is found in 1 John 2: 15–17:

> Do not love the world or anything in the world. If anyone loves the world, the love of the Father is not in him. For everything in the world—the cravings of sinful man, the lust of his eyes and the boasting of what he has and does—comes not from the Father but from the world. The world and its desires pass away, but the man who does the will of God lives forever.

There is a serious matter brought up in this passage. We are specifically told not to fall in love with the world or any of its temptations. The Apostle John was not referring to the world in the sense of natural things like forests, lakes, streams, and the other splendors we see in God's creation. He meant the things this world holds out as temptations for us—things which can take our hearts and minds off of God.

The danger in loving God's creations lies in going further than simply enjoying them; it is when we begin to lust after them that we are breaking His command. This test requires us to take a look at our inward self, and determine what motivates us to acquire worldly possessions. We also need to determine what causes us to participate in the worldly activities which we find ourselves a part of. One of the best methods for us to use in figuring out the answers to these questions is to simply ask ourselves whether or not the things we are striving for and involved with will be pleasing to God? Is the motivation of your heart something you should be ashamed of; or is it pure? Will God be glorified through your actions? The key is to look at whether or not you have this problem, and then ask God to help you to correct it if you do.

One of my own problem areas when I was younger was getting caught up in the race the world calls *keeping up with the Jones'*. I spent many extra hours at work to keep up in this rat race. Those were hours away from my family, and I can't get them back. In order to buy the biggest home possible, the newest vehicles to drive, a vacation getaway spot, and whatever else worked its way into the equation, nothing stopped me from working. I believe most of you will know what I mean, since this is a problem which plagues so many of us. It seems like, for many of us, there is no such thing as "good enough" when it comes to our possessions in life. However, once you overcome this particular stumbling block, your life can be so much simpler, and a real blessing.

It can be a fine line to see this difference between enjoying the pleasures this life can bring and worshipping them, but it is there. Can you see if you have crossed this line in your own life? Examine yourself, and see if you are going beyond a healthy enjoyment of this world. Do you have a spirit of boastfulness when sharing with someone about what you have accomplished or amassed here on earth? We are warned against falling into this position in Matthew 6:19–21:

> Do not store up for yourselves treasure on earth, where moth and rust destroy, and where thieves break in and steal. But store up for yourselves treasures in heaven, where moth and rust do not destroy, and where thieves do not break in and steal. For where your treasure is, there your heart will be also.

A true believer will have a desire to accumulate treasures, but they will desire the kinds that are pleasing to God. They will strive to serve God, and to manage their possessions in a way honoring Him. You may have a lovely home, but do you use it as a place to fellowship with other believers? Do you use it as a place to meet and look into God's Word? When someone enters your home, do they immediately know from looking around that God is the center of your life? Christians, who have been blessed by God with financial means, should bless others by sharing them. Look at yourself to determine if you are sharing your blessings with others, or are you bragging about them? There is nothing wrong with obtaining much of what this world has to offer. How you obtain it, and what you do with it, is what you need to examine. It may hurt to look, but you must if you are going to see where you stand in God's plan. You cannot love both God and the world in the same sense, so determine which of the two you love the most.

The next test we find is from 1 John 3:1–2:

> How great is the love the Father has lavished on us, that we should be called children of God! And that is what we are! The reason the world does not know us is that it did not know him. Dear friends, now we are children of God, and what we will be has not yet been made known. But we know that when he appears, we shall be like him, for we shall see him as he is.

Here we are told we need to recognize that we are children of God, and because we are His children; He loves us. We also know it is only through Jesus Christ's sacrifice on the Cross that we can become His children. Jesus promised us He will be coming back, and one of the places this is found is in Matthew 24:26–31:

> "So if anyone tells you, 'There he is, out in the desert,' do not go out; or, 'Here he is, in the inner rooms,' do not believe it. For as lightning that comes from the east is visible even in the west, so will be the coming of the Son of Man. Wherever there is a carcass, there the vultures will gather.
>
> Immediately after the distress of those days the sun will be darkened, and the moon will not give its light; the stars will fall from the sky, and the heavenly bodies will be shaken.

> At that time the sign of the Son of Man will appear in the sky, and all the nations of the earth will mourn. They will see the Son of Man coming on the clouds of the sky, with power and great glory. And he will send his angels with a loud trumpet call, and they will gather his elect from the four winds, from one end of the heavens to the other."

Jesus Christ will be coming back a second time, and all who believe will be gathered up to join Him in Heaven. The question this test poses for you is: are you looking forward to that day? This is a two-sided question for us. First, it asks us if we are looking forward to His coming because of the blessings coming to us, but it also asks if we are dreading what awaits those who are not ready for His return. These are two thoughts very much worth considering, because they both help to see where we are in God's plan.

Are you looking forward to the second-coming of Jesus? If you are, you should view that fact as another piece of evidence proving you are truly saved. If you are not, you need to determine what is keeping you from doing so. We know everyone will spend eternity either in Heaven with God, or in eternal torment through separation from Him in hell. It is quite understandable to feel apprehensive about Christ's return due to the fact that you may have loved ones who are not ready for His return, but it should not be because of your own condition. Think about your own position and decide whether or not you are looking forward to the return of our Lord.

This next test asks us whether or not we have cleaned up our life as a believer. It is found in 1 John 3:4-6; 9–10:

> Everyone who sins breaks the law; in fact, sin is lawlessness. But you know that he appeared so that he might take away our sins. And in him is no sin. No one who lives in him keeps on sinning. No one who continues to sin has either seen him or known him. No one who is born of God will continue to sin, because God's seed remains in him; he cannot go on sinning, because he has been born of God. This is how we know who the children of God are and who the children of the devil are: Anyone who does not do what is right is not a child of God; nor is anyone who does not love his brother.

This test looks at the status of our behavior in our life, and asks us if we are living a purified life. I do not mean to say it asks if we are living a life free from sin, since we know Jesus was the only one who will ever be capable of doing that. Instead, I mean have you straightened up your behavior in this life? The traits and habits you held as standards in your life before you professed to be born again; are they still present, or have they been washed clean? A good way to describe what I mean by this comes from a nineteenth century preacher named Charles Spurgeon. He defined it by claiming that the last person any true believer will ever want to meet would be themselves before their regeneration by God. So, the question this test asks is: if you could meet yourself, would you be happier with whom you are now than you the person you were before your salvation?

This question does not simply ask you to think about the obvious differences you should be able to see in your regenerated heart, such as sexual purity, faithfulness to your spouse, respect towards authority, truthfulness, and other such character traits. This test asks you to examine the less obvious traits, such as: how is your demeanor? Are you still prone to temper tantrums and fits of anger? Do you tell the truth most of the time, or do you bend it a little to suit your needs? Do you gossip with others, or talk negatively about fellow believers? These are the types of traits we should eliminate from our lives, with the help of the Holy Spirit, after we are born again.

On the other side of the coin, there are traits which can keep us from doing the things we ought to be doing. This condition is expressed in James 4:17; “Anyone, then, who knows the good he ought to do and doesn't do it, sins.” If we meditate on this verse, it may serve as a means of convicting us of our sinful behavior. An example of how I was convicted by this passage came in the area of tithing. I simply wasn’t tithing. Are you? If not; why not? I found there were two possible reasons to explain my lacking in this area. Either I loved my personal finances a bit more than I ought to, or I didn't understand how everything I have comes from God in the first place.

There are some other examples of living a purified life to consider, such as prayer. Do you spend time with God in prayer? Do you spend time in devotions reading His Word? Are you serving Him in a ministry at your church? Are you regularly attending one of His churches? Are you helping in an evangelical way by witnessing to others around you in your family and at work? These are things we should be doing as part of this cleaning process called sanctification. As you consider these questions, ask yourself if you are really cleaning up your life. If you are, mark it down as another proof of your salvation. If not, try to figure out why, and ask God to help you to change in the right ways.

Our next passage asks us a simple question, and is found in 1 John 3:14; "We know that we have passed from death to life, because we love our brothers. Anyone who does not love remains in death." If you pause to consider the message in this verse of Scripture, it can be easily understood. It says we who believe will love our fellow believers. The answer to this question is found when you examine your walk. When opportunities come up to spend time with your fellow believers, do you take advantage of them, or avoid them? I speak from experience on this condition, because it was one that convicted me when I reflected on my own status; I did not display a love for my fellow believers through my actions.

When you become aware of special needs among your fellow believers, are you someone who steps up to help them out? If you do, I congratulate you, because servant hood is one of the traits Jesus exhibited for us. We are told we must be servant-minded, and by doing this, we are behaving as Christ did. One of the places this can be found is in Philippians 2:5–8:

> Your attitude should be the same as that of Christ Jesus: Who, being in very nature God, did not consider equality with God something to be grasped, but made himself nothing, taking the very nature of a servant, being made in human likeness. And being found in appearance as a man, he humbled himself and became obedient to death—even death on a cross!

So simply ask yourself this question: do I love my fellow believers? Do I show it through my actions? Am I a willing servant when it comes to helping them out in times of trial? Do I spend time with other believers so I can be nourished and grow in my spiritual walk? An easy way to answer this question, in my own position, was to place the names of the ten people I spent the most time with, other than my family, into a list. When I did this with complete honesty, it wasn't very hard to see if the ones I spent the most time with were the same people I called fellow believers. The answer I came up with proved to be a real eye-opener for me. If when you do this, you have your eyes opened in the same way as I did, take hope in the fact you can drop to your knees and tell God you're sorry. He will hear your apology, and deliver whatever you need to overcome your downfall.

Don't get the wrong impression, and think that I am saying believers need to live in a bubble, with only other believers allowed inside with them. We are told to spread the Good News of salvation with the whole world, not just with other believers. We need to be involved with as many people who are lost as is possible for us, and to share God's plan with all of them. When it comes to the people you listed as being those with whom you spend the most time, they really need to be members of God's family. Our closest friends are the ones who influence us the most. So in order to be influenced in the most positive ways possible, these friends should be our brothers and sisters in Christ.

Our next self-exam can be a little more difficult to answer, and is found in 1 John 3:21–22; "Dear friends, if our hearts do not condemn us, we have confidence before God and receive from him anything we ask, because we obey his commands and do what pleases him." The question posed is this, do you receive answers to the prayers you offer to God? If we pause a moment to consider the depth of this question, we can see why it can be difficult to answer. It can be very difficult to know if we receive answers to the prayers we make, and some prayers may take years for us to hear the answer to them.

This passage states an important condition we need to be in before we can expect our prayers to be answered; our hearts must not be condemning us about our position in life. It also says we can have confidence in our prayers only if we are obeying God's commands, and doing what pleases Him. If we are not, our hearts should be busily condemning us. It is only after we meet these requirements that we can gain confidence in our prayers being both heard, and answered.

So what about you; are your prayers being answered? Do you have confidence when you submit them before God? When you ask for something, does it fit into God's Kingdom? Are your prayers asking for selfish things? Do you pray for things which will not be glorifying to God? Are your prayers mostly of the "let me have" type? This is something we need to consider, and then determine whether or not God is answering. If He is, then you are asking them in a way pleasing to Him. You should have unshakable confidence in the fact you will receive an answer to whatever it is you ask. If you feel like your prayers fall on deaf ears, examine what it is you are praying for and the reasons behind your prayers. We need to re-examine our lives, so we can pray with the confidence His children should have, when they obey His commands and seek to please God in all they do and say.

One more test question we can find comes from 1 John 4:1; "Dear friends, do not believe every spirit, but test the spirits to see whether they are from God, because many false prophets have gone out into the world." This exam asks if you are able to distinguish between those who teach in a manner contrary to the Word of God, and those who are sharing in a way true to God. As believers, we should gain the ability to recognize the truth from lies. Our hearts should let us know which one it is we are hearing, when someone shares from God's Word with us. No matter how sincerely something is presented to you as coming from the Word of God, when it is a falsehood, your heart should detect an error, and go off like some sort of an alarm for you.

The times have been very rare when my heart has told me that what was being taught or preached during a church service was not *right*. But there have been a few instances, and those are the times we have to conduct our own in-depth study of God's Word. We need to do this to be sure of whether the teaching is correct or not. The key is to never accept any teaching with blind obedience; always check to make sure it agrees with God's Word first!

The last question from this series is found in 1 John 4:13; "We know that we live in him and he in us, because he has given us of his spirit." Ask yourself: does the Holy Spirit live inside of you? This is a subject many I have talked with seem to want to avoid, because of its supernatural implications. Believers need the Holy Spirit in their lives. Without Him, we are all helpless before the world's temptations, and the enemy's advances. He is our guiding light. He is the one who shows us the way to victory. Without His help, we will be the victims in this battle, instead of the victors.

So how do we know if the Holy Spirit is there in our heart? What can we look for to know if He is there? What can serve as a witness of His presence? One of the ways He shows Himself is in our conscience. He lets you know when you are not behaving as you should, or if you are doing things you shouldn't be doing. He is also the source of our inspiration when we feel compelled to take on tasks to help in the advancement of God's kingdom. He won't push you into doing anything, but He will show you what you should want to do.

Each and every one of us who come to faith through Jesus Christ, have the opportunity to grow in tune with the Holy Spirit. The sad reality is that not all of us do. I went years without paying much attention to His calls, even though He was trying to help me start moving forward in my walk. Now, I am able to look back and see the many times I ignored Him, and it causes me to be ashamed. His encouragement is why I have taken the time to write this book. Whether or not God chooses to bless this book by seeing it published, I have finally stepped up and done what was laid on my heart to do. At the very least, I have grown through the writing. That alone has made it worthwhile for me. If you will follow the Spirit's guiding hand, you will find whatever you are led to do, will be rewarding for you too.

This is what I mean by the Spirit's witness in your life. Do you find yourself doing things you would have never done before? Do you find yourself reading Scripture in a class or meeting? Do you pray in public? Do you invite others to come and hear what your Pastor has to say? Are you volunteering to work in programs your church uses in ministering to the community? These are the evidences of the Holy Spirit's presence in your life. They are things people will not do in their natural state. If you find yourself participating in ways you never would have before, and you are doing things you never would have done before, it should serve as proof for you of the Holy Spirit's presence in your life, and further proof that you are listening to His guiding voice. This voice will only be heard by your inner spirit; so, listen for His whisper. Look at your life, and see if this evidence is there. Then ask yourself: is the Holy Spirit present in my life?

My last question is: are you helping or hurting? This is a question all of us who profess to be Christians need to ask ourselves. If we are absolutely honest with ourselves, we may find we don't like the answer. We must ask God to help us to correct whatever is wrong with us if we find ourselves lacking in any way. That is the point I wanted to share in this book. In the last chapter, I will share my personal feelings on what we can do to help correct these wrongs. I pray you will find something in these words to help you find God. If you are not searching for Him, I pray you will be led to start. If you are already serving Him, I pray you will find something to help you reach higher, and serve Him with an even greater passion than ever before! It is this kind of passion which has led me to write, and it can lead you to do things you never imagined possible, too!

Chapter Twelve

Can I Get a Witness!?!

One of the first thoughts coming to my mind right now is how excited I am to be nearing the completion of this project. Another is how sad I am to see it coming to its end. It has taken more than a year to complete this book, and now I will be finding out whether or not a publisher thinks it is worthy of publishing. I wish I could ask all of you to pray for this, but I am forced to settle for a group of my closest friends and fellow believers. If you find yourself reading this book, I want you to see it as another proof of God being bigger than any of us! There have been many attempts by the enemy to convince me I was wasting my time, but I have not listened to him...much. That is another proof of the power in the prayers of God's family, and I want to thank all of those who helped me in a prayerful way.

So how do I wrap up what I have been trying to share in this book? I started out wanting to address the many excuses people offer for why they don't accept Jesus Christ as their Lord and Savior, but I feel I ended up looking at much more than just a list of excuses. While trying to understand why people cling to their list of excuses instead of clinging to Christ, I have found that most of them have not met Christians whose lives could alter their thinking. We are all called to be witnesses of the truth, and professors of the reason for the hope found inside of us. We are told this in 1 Peter 3:15–16:

> But in your hearts set apart Christ as Lord. Always be prepared to give an answer to everyone who asks you to give the reason for the hope that you have. But do this with gentleness and respect, keeping a clear conscience, so that those who speak maliciously against your good behavior in Christ may be ashamed of their slander.

Those who are saved must fulfill our calling to bring others to a life with Christ. We need to turn our lights on, and let our salt rub off on the rest of the world.

This teaching comes from Jesus' Sermon on the Mount, and it is found in Matthew 5:13–16:

> You are the salt of the earth. But if the salt loses its saltiness, how can it be made salty again? It is no longer good for anything, except to be thrown out and trampled by men. You are the light of the world. A city on a hill cannot be hidden. Neither do people light a lamp and put it under a bowl. Instead they put it on its stand, and it gives light to everyone in the house. In the same way, let your light so shine before men, that they may see your good deeds and praise your Father in heaven.

There lies the answer to why the lost are not seeking and searching for God's truth. There are too many out there who are truly saved, and yet they do not listen to the Holy Spirit's guidance. If they did, they would shine so brightly before others that they could not be missed! I speak from experience; because this is a condition I was guilty of myself. After you completely surrender to the Holy Spirit's controlling influence, you will begin to see fruit produced from your walk that you never imagined was possible!

Please don't misunderstand my thoughts, and mistakenly think I am excusing those who profess to be Christians, but who do not show any evidence of Christ in their lives; I am not. I shared those tests of salvation with you so you can try to determine for yourself whether the reason for a lack of fruit in your own walk is maybe because you are just a lazy Christian, or if maybe it is because you have deceived yourself into believing a lie about your true position in God's plan of salvation. Before you can be the salt and light for this world, you will have to be assured of your own salvation. This is the matter of greatest importance any of us can bestow on anything. It is our salvation!

Before we can spend our energy in trying to help lead others to a relationship with Jesus Christ, we must know we have already received that victory in our own life. Consider the proofs I have listed, and see if they can be found as evidence of your faith; see if they ring true in your life. If they do not, you need to concentrate on your own position before you start working on someone else's. The one will automatically start taking care of the other, once you are in the right place in God's plan. By that, I mean if you are not truly saved, but are trying to help others find their salvation, you are not shining as you should in order to help them to see. If you correct this by coming to God's saving grace, then you can shine so brightly, you will make others crave what has taken hold of you; they will hunger and thirst after it.

For those of you who have been convinced of your position for a long period of time, I know it is very difficult to consider the possibility that you're anything other than what you have believed for so long. This is something which plagued me for a long time, but I forced myself to look at my reality. I knew I wasn't producing fruit for God's kingdom, no matter how hard I tried. Once in a while, God would bless one of my efforts; but it always seemed like it was in spite of me, instead of through me. I hope that makes sense to some of you who might be in the same position of misunderstanding the condition of your life as I was. I have now been given a passion for helping others to see this error, because I have seen the difference it can make in our walk when we move from a false understanding to a true one.

If you are unsure of your salvation after going through the various checklists in this book, I cannot suggest strongly enough for you to seek help in overcoming your doubt. Seek out a Pastor, a Bible teacher, or anyone else who you feel in your heart is a member of God's family, and share your thoughts with them. Let them help you to find God's truth in His Word, and pray for the Holy Spirit to help you to understand as you read them. Go back to square one, no matter how long you have thought you were already saved. No matter how many times before you tried to do the same thing; do it again. Never stop trying to achieve your salvation. We should always follow Scripture, and continue to work out our salvation with fear and trembling. None of us should ever become so self-assured that we choose to simply rest in our salvation.

I pray that all of you who are still lost will come to see the errors in your excuses for not asking God to forgive you for your sinful lives. I pray you will drop to your knees, and cry out to Him! You do not have to recite any pre-approved or scripted prayer for Him to hear you. You just have to be sincere when you cry out. If you don't feel as if God has regenerated your heart, keep crying out until you know He has! You have read about the evidences that should appear in your life after this has happened, and you should be able to recognize them in your own life when they occur.

To those who know they are already truly saved, I am speaking to you with all of my passion. It is due to the lack of obedience to God's Word on the part of many of us, that others are not being drawn to Him as they could be. For true believers, we have the witness of God's Spirit in our life. Having the Holy Spirit in our heart should be more than enough for us to be able to rise above this world and its agendas. We are without excuse, so don't make any if you are guilty of a lack of obedience. We must overcome the enemy's efforts to limit our fruitfulness, because the souls of others may depend on our helping to show them the way! Do not let the enemy toss filth on top of your light, so others can't see it!

We all wish our light had shined much sooner, but we must accept that everything is all part of God's timing. We all have regrets from missed opportunities for witnessing to others, when we failed miserably in our handling of them. Regret is something we are all familiar with. The regret which comes from having failed to show a lost sinner why they need to seek God is a type of regret I wouldn't wish on any one! I pray that others who might see this type of flaw in themselves will listen to the Holy Spirit's instructions, and be led to correct it.

We must become salty for the world's sake. When that passage from the book of Matthew was written, salt was what they used to preserve their meats to prevent rot and decay. It means the same thing for the believer; we are meant to help prevent others from going through the decaying process in their souls. We are meant to help show them a better way to live their life by living one! We cannot stand by and idly watch others as they head towards their eternal destruction—not if we are true believers! We must be an example for them. Our example can serve to help preserve their souls. This can only happen if we are salty ourselves.

The number one excuse brought up by the lost as to why they don't seek Christianity is hypocrisy. It is a huge problem for us as believers, and it takes away our saltiness. It is what the Scriptures mean when they say no one takes a candle and covers it; it is meant to shine so all those around it can see. As true believers, we must rise above this problem of saying one thing, but displaying something else in our walk. We should not remain as mere babes in God's kingdom. We must grow and mature, so we can shine brighter and brighter for this world! This is what is meant by our process of sanctification; it is our moving forward in our faith. We are to become more and more Christ-like through following God's commands and listening to the guiding voice of the Holy Spirit.

Jesus Christ's Sermon on the Mount, found in the book of Matthew chapters 5, 6, and 7, can serve to lead us in this process of sanctification. We should spend as much time as possible in these three chapters. We should meditate on where we fall in this teaching. Jesus laid out for us how we should feel as believers, and then He told us what we should be doing as believers. Many believers have grown through spending time in that sermon, and then doing their best to apply those principles in their own lives. That is something we all should do, and then we can enjoy the growth which will begin to take place in our hearts. The lost will see this growth in our walk, through the changes taking place. That is when we become the salt and light through which they can come to see their own error, and help prevent them from decaying with this world.

Once we have started down the path towards our spiritual maturity as believers; we will not want to turn back. You will find that, no matter how long you have been saved, you will still have the same burning desire to know God more closely, just like every new convert does. You will find you have more concern over how God will feel about events in your life, than you will about how other men do. You will love the gifts God will bestow upon you, more than you ever enjoyed the ones the world brought to you. You will know that God's gifts are eternal; the world's are but for a few moments in this life. This kind of knowledge will enable you to wipe the filth from your life, coming from the world's influence; then you will shine as God intended!

When trying to understand Christianity, a common mistake many believe is that Christians are only interested in things such as reading our Bibles and spending time talking about what is written in God's Word. Many think a Christian is someone who spends all of their time doing things which we call "religious." This is not what being a Christian is about at all. It is not the things you are doing and talking about which make you a Christian; it is what God has done to your heart that makes you a Christian! We do not simply decide to become a Christian, and take it up as our standard of living. Christianity takes you up, and turns you into someone new—someone you weren't before. That is what is meant by being regenerated (born again), and it comes from the power of God!

I thought for years that I had "taken up" Christianity, only to find out it had never taken me up! I had been doing all of those things like reading my Bible, talking about what I read, deciding it sounded right, and showing interest in what was written. But that was the extent of my walk, and I had remained content in my state for far too long. This book was written for those who are just like I was. Is that where you are my friend? If regardless of all of your personal efforts, you feel you are still as lost as ever, you are at the point where God can save you!

Start there, and make your salvation sure, by placing it completely into God's capable hands! That is the first step in becoming the salt needed to stall the decay gripping this world. Your life will be like shining a light into the darkest corner where evil lurks, pulling men down into its pit. Only a true believer is going to shine in a way that draws the lost to them. Then your saltiness will rub off on them, and they will want what God has given to you: forgiveness! Not perfection, but forgiveness of sins!

Perfection will not be achieved until we meet Jesus Christ in Heaven, but we can become more and more like Him through our sanctification process while we are here on earth. Our sanctification will help us to overcome any hypocrisy in our walk, as we listen to the Holy Spirit's guiding voice. We will then be able to help the lost people we meet as they see our example. We will be able to show them there is something real and powerful in what we profess, because it is evident in our life. It won't take you long to make this kind of difference, once you start down your Christian path of sanctification. It doesn't take long to shine like a powerful spotlight, especially when you compare the difference in a true believer's life against what they were when they were still lost!

There is nothing as valuable as our souls. God sent His

Son to die on the Cross for them. What else could men possess as valuable as a soul, that God would punish His Son in order to save? Nothing! So, first acknowledge the importance of your own soul, and that is where you can start your life as a soul-winner for God's kingdom. Second, invite God's Spirit to lead your life, and to guide you down the path God wants you to take. Let Him be the leading force in your life, and obey His commands.

After you know you are one of God's children, you can begin to obey His commands. You will come to see yourself being sanctified through the molding of His hands. This is as important, in my eyes, as any other step we can take. It is the step which throws salt into your soul, and turns the wattage up on your light; until it is blinding to those around you! This step will help you to rise above the state of hypocrisy, which so many professing believers are prone to collapse under. Once you start this process, you can help to erase the number one excuse of so many who are still lost in this world: hypocrisy.

A pleasant thought comes to mind from my school days, of a term used in math class—geometric progression. If you aren't familiar with this term, it has to do with how things tend to re-create themselves in progression, which causes an ever-increasing number to be generated. It means if you put two together, they split into four, then they split into eight, then they split into sixteen, and so on. Think of that math term in regards to the crop of new believers who, because of the examples of true believers, come to see their need to be regenerated by God. This comes from the parable of the sower of seeds, found in Matthew 13:3–9:

> Then he told them many things in parables, saying: "A farmer went out to sow his seed. As he was scattering

> the seed, some fell along the path, and the birds came and ate it up. Some fell on rocky places, where it did not have much soil. It sprang up quickly, because the soil was shallow. But when the sun came up, the plants were scorched, and they withered because they had no root. Other seed fell among thorns, which grew up and choked the plants. Still other seed fell on good soil, where it produced a crop—a hundred, sixty, or thirty times what was sown. He who has hears, let him hear."

I hope you share in my excitement over this passage of Scripture, as you consider the possibility of geometric progression taking place through your submitting to God's commands, and His plan for your life. If you can become one of the farmers who sows seed for God's kingdom, your efforts may yield a crop growing in just such a manner! What could be as exciting as that possibility? Nothing! So I encourage you to give it a try, and see what God has in store for you. I guarantee, you will never be able to imagine how much God can do through your life of obedience if you will just ask Him! Listen to His Spirit, and start your process of sanctification; it will be the beginning of your usefulness in His plan.

Oh, that we could all be so salty and shine so brightly, that no one could deny there was something done in us which could not have been done by mortal hands! Then those around us would have no choice but to acknowledge the vast difference between us and everyone else who is not a true believer. If we shine in such a way, the lost will stop making excuses based on the behavior of God's children. They will have to accept responsibility for their own failure to seek His forgiveness. They will be forced to accept that it is because of their own love of self and the world that they refuse to turn to God.

If you were already in God's saving grace, but you weren't shining as you ought to, I pray you have been inspired to let the Holy Spirit wipe your lens clean. Then, you will be able to shine brighter than you ever have before! If we submit to God's will in this way, many might be saved through our examples of submission. We are called to be the farmers who sow the seeds of God's kingdom. The Holy Spirit waters the seeds, and makes them grow. We are also called to be fishers of men. So, we need to learn how to cast our nets upon the waters in a way that catches men's hearts and souls.

As we become sanctified, we will see more clearly. We will shine more brightly. We will rub off on others, just as salt is rubbed into the meat to prevent decay. God will be glorified through our efforts, so I urge all of you who see yourself as a child of God; strive as never before to listen to the Holy Spirit as He guides and directs you. If you are unsure of your salvation; seek out individuals who you feel in your heart can help you to understand God's plan for your life. Work out your salvation with fear and trembling, just as Scripture tells us to do.

My prayer is for those of us who are believers, to let the Holy Spirit help to erase this condition of hypocrisy which plagues so many of us. Then, we can more easily be used by God to draw others to Himself, and His kingdom. There is nothing more valuable than our soul, and the souls of others around us. My prayer for all who profess Christianity is to turn on your light, and pass the salt...please! That is what we are told to do, and the Holy Spirit is there to give us the power to make it happen. Please, let Him do His work in your life, so you can be used to help open the door to the hearts of others around you. Help them to see the difference Jesus

Only through the power of His Spirit

Christ makes in a believer's life, so they will crave the same condition in their own! God will bless you for your obedience to His Word, and to His Holy Spirit! Amen.

About The Author

My name is Michael W. Saunders. I was born in Michigan in 1958. My parents moved to Arizona when I was two years old, and then to California when I was five. We remained there until 1971, and then moved back to Michigan.

My church life didn't begin until we moved back to Michigan, when my parents moved down the street from a Free Methodist Church. It was a smaller church with about 200 people showing up each week for worship services.

This church had an outreach program for their Sunday school service, using a bus pickup program to gather up children for their classes. My parents started putting me and my three siblings on the bus, and we went to the classes there.

Initially, we went to the morning classes, but not the worship services. This went on for our first year there, and then during my freshman year of high school, I began attending the Wednesday evening program for senior high school students. The program there was called the Free Methodist Youth (FMY) Club.

It was during this year I met my first and only sweetheart, Denise. She became my best friend, and after six years of dating we were married in this same church. We have now been happily married for twenty-nine years, and have raised two sons and a daughter. We now reside in a rural community in Michigan.

Denise and I attended Sunday School and the Free

Methodist Youth Program on Wednesdays together regularly. We also began attending Sunday morning worship services. We both felt the need to be there, and were both searching for something in our lives that was missing. We heard the salvation message, and we both responded to it.

About eight years after meeting at this church, we moved to a new community. We tried a few different churches there, and settled on a new church and denomination; we began attending a small independent Baptist church. We were attracted to this church by their friendly atmosphere and the fact they were a faith-based, Bible-preaching church, just as the Free Methodist Church had been. We enrolled our three children in the AWANA (Approved Workman Are Not Ashamed) program there, and worked as leaders for almost fifteen years. We attended church services regularly, and were as involved as any young couple with a family can be. We are still attending this church, though we moved twenty-five miles away. After searching for a new church home, we realized this was where we felt the most at home.

Although I had asked Christ to come into my heart, and for God to adopt me as one of His children nearly thirty years earlier, I still felt something was missing in my life. I felt like this even though I had done the things I believed I was supposed to. I went to church, I worked in children's programs, I read my Bible, I prayed; yet I knew something was missing.

I felt this way until four years ago, when an evangelist came and conducted a four-day revival at our church. I was inspired by him to read some books on spiritual depression, and I was convicted in an area of my life I had never understood before.

Although I had received Jesus Christ in my heart as my Savior, I had never surrendered complete control of my life to the Holy Spirit. After much thought and prayer on this new conviction, I immediately began to see changes in myself, and the way I saw the people around me changed too.

One of these changes has been a strong desire to help others who need to find their salvation. This was an area I had never been active in before. As far as witnessing went, I had never done it. After talking to other believers, I found this is an area many of us have never been very involved in. It has become one of the areas in my life I am now the most passionate about. I have tried to figure out why it is so hard for most of us to witness, and how we can become more active in this area, just as Jesus told us to be.

This new commitment to Christ I made four years ago has lead me to this new point in my life. I am now trying to help others see the importance of witnessing. I have asked the Holy Spirit to lead and guide me to be used to the best of my God-given gifts and abilities in all areas of my life, especially in helping lead others to their salvation.

I feel the Spirit has given me insight into some of the things making it so difficult for myself and other believers to share our faith with others. He has also shown me some of the reasons why we have so much difficulty accepting our own salvation. Friends have told me I have a gift of being able to share my feelings in a way easy for them to understand. In the past, they had felt my passion when I shared about the things I loved doing with them—things like bowling, fishing, exercising, or any other "ings." Now, the "ings" I feel passionate about are: praying, witnessing, fellowshipping, and worshipping.

I have a burning desire to share the ideas in this book with others, as well as the wonderful difference it makes when we place Jesus Christ as the Lord of our life and the Savior of it. I am available to appear as a witness and motivational speaker at camps, seminars, revivals, and church services.

I can be contacted by email at:

fieldhandministries@yahoo.com

It is my hope and prayer that you might gain some insight from my observations, and for them to help you in your personal walk with Christ. That was my motivation in sitting down and writing this book. I am praying for God's guidance, and praying others may grow from this effort. It is all for the glory of our Father in Heaven, Amen.

To order additional copies of *What's Your Excuse?*, or to find out about other books by Michael Saunders or Zoë Life Publishing, please visit our website www.zoelifepub.com.

A bulk discount is available when 12 or more books are purchased at one time.

Contact Outreach at Zoë Life Publishing:

Zoë Life Publishing
P.O. Box 871066
Canton, MI 48187
(877) 841-3400
outreach@zoelifepub.com

ZOË LIFE PUBLISHING
WORDS TO LIVE BY